For Mary Van Pelt, the "marginalized" of this world are not an abstraction. *After the Murder* takes us into a reality that is both intensely foreign and intimately familiar. She shows us the reality of exterior and interior prisons, and the brokenness and transformation to be found there. Through Mary's willingness to face her own pain, and the pain of a man she has loved for much of her life, she guides us through the turbulent waters of love's power to wound, to heal, to preserve and to release.

—The Rev. Katherine Griffis
Alamosa Presbyterian Church

Other books by
Mary Elizabeth Van Pelt

In Silence I Speak

ๆ๒๒๒๒๒

www.maryvanpelt.com

After the Murder

my affair with a felon

Mercury HeartLink

After the Murder

my affair with a felon

Mary Elizabeth Van Pelt

After the Murder: my affair with a felon
Copyright ©2011 Mary Elizabeth Van Pelt

ISBN: 978-0-9827303-6-2
Publisher: Mercury HeartLink

Book design by Mercury HeartLink
Back cover portrait photograph by Miles Eddy

This is a memoir. The names of people, places and other identifying characteristics have been changed.

Mercury HeartLink
www.heartlink.com
editor@heartlink.com

For additional copies and other books by Mary Elizabeth Van Pelt go to: *www.maryvanpelt.com*

For information regarding speaking engagements and other projects contact the author at: *mary@maryvanpelt.com*

Contents

Acknowledgments

About the Author

Publisher's Note

Established in 1994, Mercury HeartLink evolved from HeartLink Integration Therapy, a family systems counseling practice and healing events enterprise. At that time activities were expanded to include Internet based projects and printing solutions that foster humanistic values and creative access to information.

As an alternative to large commercial publishing houses, and the unguided and less professional endeavors of self-publishing, Mercury HeartLink works closely with writers and other artists to offer solutions that are client-centered and provide support in the larger realm of self-realization.

Mercury HeartLink welcomes individual and collaborative works of educational, cultural and community value. These may include creative non-fiction, fiction, memoir and poetry, but all have two things in common: an authenticity on the part of the author and a responsibility to positive social impact. It is with enthusiasm then that Mercury HeartLink accepts another opportunity to present the work of Mary Elizabeth Van Pelt.

After the Murder begins with a personal story and ends with letters. Van Pelt's affair with a felon begins with letters and never ends. So, too, our quest for love, justice and redemption. I invite the reader to examine the evidence: the author's narrative and the letters of a convicted murderer. There is no final judgment required—the sentencing by society of the offender (and to a large degree, also his lover) has already occurred. The issues that remain, however, are central to our survival.

Those who are squeamish when presented with ambiguities and shaky when exploring their own values and human fallibilities have made their call and moved on. But the courageous will remain, not out of duty nor idle intrigue with suffering, but because they, like Coretta Scott King, have come to the end of justification—the last door. And the last door is always the entry into the heart of who we are, and who we might become. Van Pelt's courageous book is a hallway that can lead the reader to that door.

—Stewart S. Warren, Albuquerque

Forgiving violence does not mean condoning violence. There are only two alternatives to forgiving violence: revenge, or adopting an attitude of never-ending bitterness and anger.

For too long we have treated violence with violence, and that's why it never ends.

—Coretta Scott King

To the murderer and
to the family of the victim,
both are suffering,
both are afraid,
both are human.

Convict Hill

Convict Hill.   People don't come here very often.   This is desolate gravel and cacti land where condemned men lie in forgotten graves and outlaw secrets and dreams of freedom are buried underground. As the story goes, the graves were marked with wooden crosses but woodpeckers destroyed them.   Now the sites are marked with rusting tags stamped out like license plates. The oldest tags have no names or dates, only the letters DOC for Department of Corrections. There's a flame of social justice or maybe just plain humanity that calls me to care about people that no one likes, living or dead—the unwanted, the people cast off by our throw away society.   Over the years I've gotten to know some of the stories like the one about Frank Tongo. Tongo was a salesman and immigrant convicted of murdering his pregnant wife and three children after it was discovered he had had an incestuous relationship with his daughter. He was the last one executed by hanging in this state, it happened before I was born. I read about him at the prison museum and then one day I came across his marker, here on the hill, shot full of rusting bullet holes.

Prisoners were buried here from the late 1800s until some time in 1970. A friend who lived in the nearby town showed me this cemetery twenty years ago. Since then I've come here many times. There's a cement slab where I sit with a view of the prison less than a mile away. I like the solitude on this hill. I sit here among the metal markers and dry weeds with sharp thorns and I think about the past, the present, the future. I think about the cycle of birth, life and death. I think about my life and then I allow my thoughts to radiate out to other lives that have touched mine or that I have touched. Sometimes I enter that meditative space where I have no thoughts, just a sense of well-being beyond the daily worries of health, love, and money. I watch as a raven glides across the open sky. I've heard it said that people often return to the site where a transformation took place. This cemetery with a view of the prison is as close as I can get to the place where my life was transformed.

The first cell house was built around the time of the Civil War when this state was still a territory. Looking west you can see the place where stone blocks were cut from the mountain to build the prison. Kiowa Correctional Facility is the place where Mark and I met.

My name is Mary. Thirty-three years ago I got on this ride, a journey through time with Mark. I was twenty-four when we met; he was twenty-six. Since the beginning it has been primarily a relationship of written words and letters. I counted the letters I received from Mark: 1,453. They fill a dozen or more large shoe boxes in my closet. It's impossible to count the ones I sent but my estimate is well over 2,000.

I began writing letters to men in prison forty years ago, although at the time I didn't know I was embarking on a life-long adventure. It was simply a way for a shy young woman to connect with a guy. I couldn't see the stigma that would follow me or that in time I would quit talking about my relationship with Mark altogether because the assumptions that people made left me feeling the huge gap between the inside world and the outside world and I didn't have the energy to constantly defend my love.

It all began with a television show. Every night for a week at the end of the evening news they showed a few minutes—an interview with an inmate named John Mitchell. I don't really know the administration's motivation behind inviting cameras into this locked and condemned world but I always suspected it was to show that prisoners were treated humanely. We were given a virtual tour. John showed us around the medium security unit and talked about the vocational training program. At the end of that week his address was posted and I wrote. That's how I began.

John and I had been writing for four years when I moved to Elmwood, a college town in the southwest. John asked if I had a girlfriend who could write his friend, Mark. I gave Mark's name to my college roommate, Gina. When I saw the letter Gina received I knew that Mark could write. I mean really write, not just parrot back short remarks like, "I'm glad you had a good time at the festival." His letter was handwritten in neat capital letters with original thoughts and ideas not numbed by years in prison. Before I met the man I was attracted to his writing.

Gina got her name approved on Mark's visiting list and together we made the three hour drive for a Saturday morning date at Kiowa Correctional Facility. At the prison we went through the check-in ritual, filled out forms and presented our drivers' licenses. We waited through moments of silent tension, fearing rejection, and then breathed a joint sigh of relief when the guard verified our names on the list. Next we were instructed to remove our shoes and stand in line for the pat down. I stood before a female guard named Hannah with my arms stretched out like a cross. Starting at my wrists the guard slid her hands up my arms and then down my back pausing at the ridge under my shirt to make sure it was nothing more than my bra fastener. Then she placed her hands on my shoulders, brought them forward like the letter V between my breasts slowing to make certain no foreign object was hidden in my bra. Her hands moved across the elastic under my bra, then around my waist, and down the outside seam of my jeans. In a final frisking motion her hands moved from mid-thigh down the inside seam of my pants. "Open your mouth." Hannah peered inside. "Touch the roof of your mouth with your tongue." When I was cleared the guard nodded and waved her hand motioning me toward the visiting room. That was the pat down search when the visitor wasn't suspected of concealing or smuggling. If a visitor was suspect she was asked to step into a private room for a more thorough search. A few years later at a different facility I saw that happen. I was detained in the visitor processing area along with five other women. We watched as two female guards ushered one visitor into a back room. The women left standing with me speculated about the body cavity search that might be happening as valuable minutes of our Sunday visit time melted away. One woman said a medical doctor was required if they were going to conduct a body cavity search. We wondered. We waited. I never found out what happened in that sequestered room although I suspect some type of humiliation. After the in-depth search the visitor suspected of a violation returned to the processing area. She was allowed to see her man. The long wait was a somber experience and reinforced the power line between prison guards and prison visitors.

At my first visits more than thirty years ago I don't recall walking through a metal detector; those came a few years later. The guard may have used a handheld wand—that's vague in my memory. The stamp of ultraviolet ink on the back of my left hand was also added to the entrance ritual in later years. At the end of a visit I passed through the processing area again, stood in line, and reached my hand beneath a black light. The ultraviolet glow proved I had properly checked in and was cleared to leave. Although it sounds absurd as I remember and write these words—I think the stamp proved that I was not an inmate disguised as a visitor and attempting to escape.

Some people called the pat down searches invasive; to endure the process I stared into the distance and went numb. This was part of the entrance routine and if I wanted to visit I had to go through it. I knew that the inmates had it worse, a strip search at the end of each visit. Mark once wrote about the humiliating procedure in a letter:

Take off your shoes and socks, your pants and shirt, your t-shirt and underwear. Stand before me, open your mouth, run your fingers behind your lips, across your gums. Now show me your hands, above your head, front and back. Show me behind your ears, run your fingers through your hair, lift your penis, your nut sack. Turn around and bend over, spread your cheeks, cough. Get dressed, return to your cell house, and report to your station in life.

In the visiting room at Kiowa there was a long row of window frames without glass. Visitors and inmates were assigned to windows. There was a ledge beneath each window just wide enough to rest my elbows. Beneath the ledge a cement wall created a barrier between those confined inside and those confined outside. The room smelled of Pine-Sol. Metal chairs echoed as they scraped across the cement floor. Other visitors in the room were mostly women and a few children. A metallic sounding message vibrated through the PA system, "Inmate four-three-nine-seven-one report to medical."

At this visit Gina met Mark for the first time and I visited John. That was the first time I laid eyes on Mark, September of 1979. I was attracted to his gentle smile. His brown hair had a tinge of red and brushed his shoulders. He had hazel eyes, strong broad shoulders, and wore a neatly trimmed beard. Like all prisoners he was dressed in the state-issued green uniform. I was attracted, but his visit was with Gina and mine was with John.

Gina and Mark had a cordial relationship but if there were any romantic feelings they were short lived. Gina left college after her first semester in the dorm and I don't know what happened to her. I mailed a Christmas card to Mark and he answered. That's how we began.

If you asked Mark how we met the story would be more colorful. "I was living next door to John Mitchell, The Phantom Rapist. John always had visitors so I asked him to put me in touch with someone. Gina and Mary came to visit, but I didn't have eyes for Gina. Mary said that I could actually write words and sentences, give feelings and impressions. She drew me into her world by describing people in her life, road trips and what she was doing. She made it real."

My first visit with Mark, after Gina lost interest and moved on, was at Kiowa Correctional Facility in

January of 1981. Kiowa is the place where my life was rescued, saved from being forever ordinary. Mark was on restriction for some infraction so our first visit was on the closed-circuit phones. We saw each other through Plexiglas. We could have matched palms and fingers with the glass separating us but even that form of virtual touch was too revealing for me—this being our "first date." I felt relieved by the physical barrier.

When I wrote letters in the privacy of my dorm room, I was a school girl consumed by the euphoria of love, but I wasn't ready to deal with the physical reality of touch, wasn't ready to transfer in love on paper to in love in person. I was anxious just thinking about the meeting. If this had been a contact visit the opportunity for a first kiss wouldn't have been spontaneous. The appointed time would have come at the end of the visit when the guard barked, "Visiting is over. Say your goodbyes."

We had explored deep waters in our letters, each one more revealing than the last. Through written words we had engaged in a playful, tempting and sensual dance until we were practically naked on the page. Now we had to face each other in a prison visiting room—*Oh my God.* A barred gate jolted, cranked horizontally, then echoed as steel slammed against steel and locked behind me. We were in a room with strangers, governed by a list of rules. This wasn't exactly a first date with the romance of a candlelit dinner in a fine restaurant. The situation was nerve-wracking enough without the possibility of a public kiss. I was glad for the Plexiglas. We talked about ordinary things: my school life, his prison life. He turned on the humor and the charm. We flirted. I swooned. He wanted me to like him. I did, desperately, absolutely and wholeheartedly. That was our first visit at Kiowa more than thirty years ago.

Thinking back upon my earlier years I see that I was not an unlikely candidate for this long distance romance. It's really more common than people might think, especially for an introvert like myself. The pattern in my life goes back to grade school. The first time I fell in love was second grade. Keith and I hid in the garage, protected by empty boxes, and explored naked things. Then my family moved from the city to a small town and I left behind my second grade lover. In my old school there were twenty-two sixth grade students. In my new school there were two thousand junior and senior high school students. I was terrified by all the unknowns. Big city confusion swirled about me like a whirlwind of loose pages and dry leaves. I felt lost, alone and helpless.

Our house sat on a busy corner and my bedroom window faced street-side. Constant traffic kept me from sleeping soundly; I stirred with each passing car. Sometimes I lay awake for hours. During sleepless times I remember asking God, over and over, to reunite me with my second grade love.

I recognized Keith the moment he walked into the classroom on that first day of seventh grade, but he didn't recognize me. Four years had passed. When the teacher called his name my heart stopped in my throat and I froze.

Had my prayer ritual really drawn him to me? There were two thousand students and here we were in the same room. I spent the next two years choreographing "chance" encounters; if I timed it just right between classes we'd pass in the hallway. I never spoke to him. Did he even know who I was?

One day I got off the bus at Keith's stop, followed him to the alley. When I opened my mouth to speak I couldn't stop trembling, there were no words. Finally, I was able to call out "Hey!" and stutter words different from the ones I'd rehearsed a thousand times.

"I kn-knew you in se-second grade and I won-wondered if you re-remem-member me."

He replied, "Yeah, but I wouldn't tell anyone about it," then he turned and walked away.

He was my long, lost love––but I wasn't his. I went home and sobbed uncontrollably for hours.

&ppb;&ppb;&ppb;&ppb;&ppb;&ppb;&ppb;&ppb;&ppb;&ppb;

During my years in a Nebraska farm town with twenty-two students in my class, I developed another distant love. Mike was the boy least liked and therefore the easiest one to befriend. The most popular boys were, in my mind, unattainable. It was a similar scenario, aside from the fact that we once danced together at Karen Johnson's birthday party, he barely acknowledged me. He knew I liked him because one of my girlfriends told him so, and at age twelve that was good enough for me. Mike wasn't very bright. He lived on a farm, came from a big family with nine brothers and sisters, and he didn't bathe very often. To put it another way he lived in deprivation and poverty. This part of the story wouldn't matter much except for what comes next.

Last summer I went back to visit that small farm town. I arranged to meet my best friend Cathy at a restaurant named Family Connections. We hadn't seen each other for twenty years, maybe longer. I have a black and white school picture of our sixth grade class and I took it with me. Cathy identified each of our former classmates: Martha became a dental hygienist; Gail got pregnant, married at age 17 and never divorced; David went into the Air Force. When she came to Mike she said, "He went to prison for molesting his stepdaughter." Cathy knew Mike was the one I liked. She paused for a moment and looked me in the eye with an unspoken, "Yes, it's true," and then continued with her litany of what happened to whom.

When I was in fourth grade Cathy lived just down the block and across the street from our house. She was like a sister to me. We had the same teachers and the same school projects. Sometimes on a Saturday morning we would walk into town and buy doughnuts, sometimes we would wander through the cemetery where pioneer tombstones dated back to the early 1800s. Together we fell in love with The Monkees—both the television program and their music. We wrote adoring fan letters and each of us received a large promotional postcard from Los Angeles with a photo of the band. For several years after my family moved to the city Cathy and I stayed in touch through letters. After graduation from separate high schools, in separate worlds, we drifted apart.

At the restaurant last summer, when Cathy told me Mike went to prison for molesting his step-daughter, she didn't know a thing about my prison relationship with Mark. I could say that hearing the information about Mike felt eerie, but really it was more of an unveiling. In sixth grade I chose a would-be boyfriend who went to prison. It was uncanny. Long before I met Mark Thompson I had a pattern of long distance romance with boys who became men living on the edge of trouble, if they hadn't already fallen in.

Stick-up Slaying

I haven't revealed the reason Mark is in prison. I wasn't there. I didn't even know Mark at the time.

But sometimes in my mind's eye I travel to another place in time where I see the murder happening as if it were a news clip. It's a cloudy day in December 1977. Two men enter a liquor store and demand cash. The victim is forced into the restroom. Then, the thrust of a knife through human flesh. Blood pools on the floor. I see Mark's life tumbling into the abyss as the spirit of George Davis leaves this world. With bloody money and booze Mark and his accomplice leave in a drunken panic. Customers discover the victim. Emergency vehicles with sirens and flashing lights arrive. News of the murder spreads like a grass fire through the small town.

Over the years I've thought about the moment that forever changed the life of the Davis family and Mark's life. I've thought about the nebulous plan for some quick cash that turned into hard time for murder. Mark's life was already lost and empty, rolling downhill, tearing through a web of shallow relationships. It finally found a place to stop. The place it stopped was that liquor store in the middle of nowhere, on the edge of Prairie County. On that bloody afternoon in Prairie County something stopped alright, but a whole new life began, one that included me.

At a prison visit Mark told me he didn't even know he had killed someone until he saw the newspaper headline the next day, December 15th, and learned that George Davis, age 62, had died. Mark called an attorney and turned himself in. Davis left behind a wife and two children, Daniel and Josephine. "I remember that day vividly," Daniel said. "I remember the worst part was having to tell my mom." I read those words in a January 2011 interview. The victims are understandably hurt and angry over the sudden brutal murder of their father. I don't pretend to know the depth of their sorrow, their suffering and their grief. I know only a few facts about their lives. But I do know the man accused and convicted of the murder. He is my friend. We fell in love but never married. Mark Thompson is the man who wrote me letters.

৵৶ ৵৶ ৵৶ ৵৶ ৵৶ ৵৶

My passion for activism, social justice and redemption; and my belief that generosity and kindness are often found in unlikely places, comes from my Calvinist roots. Although we didn't call ourselves missionaries, we were missionaries. That's the world I was born into. My father was a Presbyterian minister educated in Kentucky and my mother was everyone's optimistic and tireless supporter. Dad worked for the People's Mission Project.

For me the word "missionary" carries stigma. It brings to mind the bloody history of one group of people trying to conquer another in the name of God. It brings to mind an annoyance, someone knocking at my door with a pamphlet and a speech while I'm in the middle of cooking dinner. Missionary carries the idea of me listening kindly to someone trying to talk me into something I don't believe, or someone carrying an unwelcome message. And then my mind leaps forward from a missionary delivering an unwanted message to a missionary being an unwanted person. Unwanted like a "drug addict," or "mental patient," or "murderer," so I don't use the word "missionary" very often.

We were rather unconventional missionaries. We didn't go door to door with Bibles and religious pamphlets carrying a message of salvation. You wouldn't see us dressed differently or behaving out of the ordinary. We didn't draw attention to ourselves by praying aloud over a meal in a restaurant. We did quiet charitable works to help disenfranchised and marginalized people. We reached out to the "less fortunate," the "disabled," and the "poor."

I was born into the privilege of middle class and the privilege of money set aside for my college education. We always had food, clothing, and a decent home. My parents took an active interest in their children's education. Birthdays and Christmases were celebrated with gifts. We took family vacation trips in a Vista Cruiser station wagon with a sun dome. I was also born into an unbalanced world, witness to giving and doing for others, and self-sacrifice, but I didn't learn about receiving until later in life. When I say "receiving"

I'm not referring to material things, but to less tangible internal things like a sense of identity and a sense of self-worth. By the time I was in my twenties my life was defined by other people's wants and needs and I'd lost track of my own, or maybe I never even knew my wants and needs.

I'm beginning to understand the judgments that we hear. Professionals say that we—women who love men in prison and women who love men who kill—are afraid of having a real relationship, that we have poor self-esteem, and that we live in a fantasy world. They say that we only "think" we are in love. We are called codependent, a label that comes with a long list of character flaws and anxiety disorders. Sometimes we are labeled *borderline personalities* because, they say, we have unstable moods, unstable relationships, and that we are manipulative and self-destructive. The list of diagnoses also imply that we are empty and don't know ourselves. Perhaps there is some truth to this emptiness, this lack of self, but how can all these faults be explained as a deficiency to someone who has never known anything else? I had to grow beyond the destructive behaviors and the criticism before it started to make sense. I'm not saying that I agree with the judgments but I've made an effort to understand where they came from. It's a chicken or egg dilemma. Does the clinical diagnosis make the isolation and emptiness worse? Does it pound us deeper into the ground? Sometimes without realizing it we build a wall around our feelings and dive head first into the self-imposed boundary of exclusion. Prison mirrors this exclusion. It is an unacceptable and isolated community largely misunderstood and harshly judged by everyday people in the outside world who make assumptions about things they don't know. It's interesting that women who are isolated within themselves, myself included, often find companionship with men who are isolated from society. We will go to extraordinary measures to protect and maintain our relationships, relationships that by their very nature always present one more new barrier. Back then, back at the beginning, I didn't think I was doing anything extraordinary or unusual; I was just living a life that made sense. My pain and my fears melted when I found someone who truly understood as no one before ever had. Contrary to popular belief I didn't fall in love with a murderer; I fell in love with a writer.

ๅๅๅๅๅๅๅๅๅ

When I reflect upon how I got into this, writing and visiting men in prison, there's another memory that comes to me. I must have been about thirteen or fourteen when I saw *Birdman of Alcatraz*. It's a 1962 film inspired by the life of a violent prison inmate named Robert Stroud who, while in captivity, studied and raised birds. In the movie he uses a piece of wire and a flame to etch and then break the neck from a glass bottle. Then he smoothes the rough edge of the broken glass on the cement floor of his cell and makes a cup so a sparrow can drink water. Over all these years why has that scene remained so vivid? The ingenuity of creating something from nothing in such a stark environment captured my imagination. The movie has many violent scenes, but it's the moment of gentleness that stuck with me.

I was strongly influenced by my Dad's work and the interesting stories he told about people. I might have been in fourth grade when Dad told me about a man in East Tennessee—sometime in the 1950s when there weren't paved roads or electricity in the back hills, and before telephone lines were installed. The man had a still and sold moonshine. During an hour of great need in the life of the church this man made an anonymous donation. "You never know who the angel might be," my father said.

And then there was the time when we lived in Alaska. Dad bought an arctic fox pelt from an Inuit hunter so that the man could have money to buy Christmas presents for his family. The white fox became lore in our family. Mother wore it on special occasions. This wasn't just fur; this was the entire fox with a soft bushy tail, four dangling legs, face, nose, and shiny black glass eyes. As a five year old this fox was especially fascinating. Under the fox's snout, where the teeth and jaw had been, was a long white clip. Attached to a rear leg hung a braided white cord and ball. To hold the fur in place around a woman's shoulders the fox's mouth clipped to the cord on his leg.

My father, the story teller, once hid the pelt behind the pulpit. I don't know how this fox fit into the sermon, but he made it work. He told the story of how the fox was captured as it ran alongside a dogsled. Then, at the perfect moment, he swooped the floppy white fox from behind the pulpit and held it high. The congregation gasped. I'm not saying the dogsled capture was true, I'm just saying it was the story that went with the fox.

Years later, back in the lower forty-eight, the white fox continued as a show and tell object when mother taught children about life in Alaska. As the daughter of a preacher I heard behind-the-scenes-stories about the congregation, stories that were not repeated outside of the home. I felt Native Alaskan and Suburban Anglo cultures clash when the fox attracted negative talk about animal rights. I was frequently aware of stories like this one that had a dual message. I witnessed acts of compassion, generosity and kindness from one side (like helping the Inuit man buy Christmas gifts for his family) that were viewed from the other side with indignity (cruelty to animals must be prevented).

From an early age I knew there were two sides to every story, and frequently more than two sides. Generally, I resolved differences passively, by listening and not arguing—not taking a side—but I knew the arctic fox story demonstrated the importance of people. It was about recognizing cultural differences, about caring for disenfranchised people, and about protecting an endangered way of life. Growing up I learned that marginalized and minority people deserved to be treated with the same dignity and respect as people like us who had social advantages. I also learned that interesting people could be found in unlikely places.

Looking back on my life I've begun to develop a new understanding. I think about the environment I was raised in: the wholesome White middle class family, the good home, the value placed on religion and education, and the emphasis placed on caring about and for others. My circumstances when combined with my own fragile sense of self, my independent way of thinking, and my somewhat rebellious nature practically lead me down the path to fall in love with Mark Thompson.

Love Letters

I still know the combination to my mailbox from thirty years ago: right H; left A; right J; then twist the latch open. I found a letter from Mark almost every day except holidays and weekends. Sometimes the mail would back up and I'd receive two or three letters at once. I suppose there was an addictive quality to the letters, to the intense feelings, and to the man—the emotional high of receiving a letter and the bummed out disappointment when more than two days passed without news.   Mail arrived in the late afternoon and I'd take it upstairs to my dorm room on the third floor. I filled with breathless anticipation each time I carefully slit open an envelope; I treated the paper as if it were sacred. I liked it best when I was alone, when my feelings weren't interrupted by a roommate opening closet doors, closing drawers or wanting to talk. Noise kept my awareness on the surface and didn't allow me to sink into my luxurious pool of blissful emotions. I'd sit at my desk reading Mark's letters over and over again, aching with desire for all that I thought possible. I didn't always read his letters right away. Sometimes I'd allow them to wait on my desk in anticipation. I'd straighten up the room, arrange my homework, brew a fresh cup of coffee and allow the energy of the letter to radiate until I could no longer resist its lure. Each letter from Mark was special like going out on a date.

We were two people starved for a meaningful human connection. Our letters were a place where I felt safe to share all of life's experiences. It was safe to swim naked through deep water; Mark wasn't afraid of my pain. Every morning for two months I wrote about the isolation and self-absorption I once lived, my memories during my time of teenage starvation. I sent this series, called *Anorexic Notes*, to Mark. Through the sensitive compassion of a man convicted of murder my old wounds began to heal. He saved those handwritten notebook pages which later became the foundation for my exploration into eating disorders.

Sometimes I'd carry Mark's most recent letter with me slipped between the pages of a textbook. I also carried the shame and guilt of a forbidden relationship. The same feelings that I knew then return to me now as I write. The fear that I betrayed my family by falling in love with a felon, the fear of disapproval, the fear that my love is harmful to others, and the fear that someone will try to force us apart. These fears have plagued me for many years.

Weekends at college were long and empty. Few students stayed on campus and there weren't many activities. On Saturdays I often walked into town. I would window shop on Main Street and then sit alone by a window in the coffee shop. I'd get buzzed on caffeine and compose another delightfully long letter to Mark. I'd write about my surroundings: the pressed tin ceiling, the black and red linoleum floor, the waitress and the weather. I'd write about school: my classes, my teachers and my assignments. I'd write my hopes and my fears. I'd reread Mark's recent letters and then respond to the conversation. On those solitary days I wrote more words than I ever spoke to anyone. I can't imagine how I would have made it through those lonesome weekends without our on-going and in-depth discussions on paper.

Sunday afternoons were the longest and my roommate was often away. Aching for Mark I'd curl into a fetal position under my patchwork quilt. In my mind I'd conjure up my last prison visit with Mark and crave his touch. I had the hormones of a young woman hungry to conceive and nurture; my breasts yearned and throbbed to suckle an infant. Regardless of people who gently suggested that Mark was an "inappropriate partner," my biological physiology was calling me to mate and the person I was opening to was a convict with eighteen years until parole. In retrospect I suppose I was making my own convoluted decision about motherhood—my decision not to bear children. I resisted the familiar path of career, marriage and family traveled by most women.

With hesitation I touch the edge of this taboo subject with my pen: the power of sexual attraction. I remember huddling over a page of thin, fine quality writing paper. Although no one else was in the room I still felt threatened by my own desire. My arms protected the words of my pen from view. I dared to write of a candle-scented room, soft shadows on the wall, and expressed my hunger to touch his body. I wrote something erotic, something lustful. Even if I could remember more details I wouldn't write them here. Just writing these few words makes me feel uneasy. I asked Mark to tear it up and throw it away after he read it. He wrote back to say he did that; he tore it to pieces and threw it away. And, he said my words were beautiful. I smiled when I recently read through our first year of letters and found that reference. I was reminded of how deeply we trusted each other with intimate feelings.

In a journal entry during my last semester of college I wrote: "I visit Mark to find out if I'm living an illusion. The visit only confirms my belief that he is the one I love." Then I asked myself, "How much of Mark will prison destroy before he is released?" And in the journal I considered the barriers between us: "One hundred and forty miles, cement walls, steel bars, gun towers, razor wire, locked doors and armed guards. Time. All of these things keep us apart. And although there is longing, hurting, missing, at least I am feeling something; at least I am not numb inside."

Until I came across that journal entry about the barriers I'd forgotten that I'd recognized them such a long time ago. It's a loop. Hope-Dream-Longing-Barrier-Isolation. No matter how many years I waited, hoped, dreamed, and believed, we always encountered another barrier. When I look at this dynamic now I feel like defending myself by saying that a woman in love who is dreaming about her future doesn't see the pitfalls she will later come to understand.

The Question of Marriage

It was a few months before my graduation from college. Ute Mountain Correctional Facility (located twelve miles east of Kiowa) was new and we were in the visiting room. This was before the ban on smoking. Visitors were allowed to bring an unopened pack of cigarettes. I bought Camel straights—the kind without a filter. Mark blew smoke rings and my eyes danced; I didn't know anyone else who could do that. We talked about marriage. We had known each other two years and his parole date was 1998, nearly twenty years away. No matter how hard I tried I couldn't see my life in 1998. The distant future was, in my mind, a blank screen. I was twenty-something, my world shifting from college to first apartment and into a new job.

Marriage to a life sentence? I mean, someone who is doing *time for life*. Why? What would marriage give us that we didn't already have? Some states allow married prisoners to have conjugal visits, but this wasn't one. The marriage question seems just as relevant today as it did thirty years ago. If we had married I think we would not have continued our journey as friends. I can't imagine the marriage would have lasted. The things that would have separated us, most likely, would have been my need to build a life outside of prison culture. Even bigger than that was my loyalty to my family. I could get away with writing letters, visiting and falling in love, but marriage was a line that would have severed connections.

The decision not to marry was clear. It was not a difficult one. It was a decision to stay on my side of the river. Crossing over would have meant entering a life on the fringe, a life I couldn't survive. I knew the tough street-wise women who visited every weekend. Their week days were focused on getting enough gas money to get to the prison, and it seemed they were barely getting by in every other way. I decided that caring about the multi-faceted issues of oppression and injustice didn't mean I had to marry into the family. So I didn't.

Saying "no" to a prison marriage didn't stop me from silently dreaming about the possibility of marriage in the future, after he got out. I saw a program on television about Common Ground Prison Reform. In my vision we would be like Gordon and Susan Hamilton, the couple in California. She's a former lower court judge; he was doing a life sentence for homicide when they met. He was released. They formed a non-profit for prison reform. Their story was a source of inspiration. I thought Mark and I could be like them. Mark would become a public speaker for prison reform, talking about social justice and deterring youth from crime. He would be a sought after legal consultant, a role model for reintegrated prisoners, and someone who understood the problems behind keeping a family together when the father is in prison. All that, maybe someday, in the future.

My maybe-someday-in-the-future dream was interrupted when Mark announced his engagement to Jasmine. They met through a mutual friend and fell in love through long distance calls. She lived in Arizona but was moving across state lines to be closer to Mark. "This won't change anything between us," Mark repeatedly reassured me in his letters. They were married by speaker phone in December of 1990. That year his Christmas card was distinctly distant, signed: "Warm Regards, Mark and Jasmine." In March of 1991 I received the never-write-to-me-again rejection letter. "My family is complete," Mark wrote. He wished me happiness in my future. I was saving space for him in my future and he shut me out.

During the two years Mark and I didn't write to each other because he was married to Jasmine, I tried to fill the gaping hole in my heart—tried to find another Mark. First I took the straight and narrow route. I wrote a letter to the prison chaplain introducing myself and stating my interest in corresponding with an inmate. A few weeks later the chaplain responded saying he usually didn't condone prisoner relationships with outside women but in this case he would make an exception. He gave my address to a young man, a good Christian from the Philippines.

Luis and I exchanged letters for a year. He was an artist. I sent him a picture of me and my sister. He made a detailed pencil drawing from the photo and wrote, "How's everything? I hope this picture finds you and your family in excellent health. Take care. My best regards to your sister. Always, Luis." Luis and I never met in person. His letters were always sincere, but I didn't find the depth I needed for a lasting connection. I was bored. At some point I received a nice-careful-polite letter that I just couldn't answer one more nice-careful-polite time. I let him fade away.

If you are a writer and you want to write someone in prison you need to find someone who can write. I did better the next time. "Control Unit Madness" appeared in *Prison Life Magazine.* The author pulled me into his insane and violent world with poignant words that showed a human being locked inside. His essay concluded with the statement, "Prison perpetuates the cycle of hatred and violence." I wrote to the editor of *Prison Life* in New York City, included an envelope with postage, and asked the editor to put me in touch with the author. A few weeks later I received a letter from Bonz (he pronounced it Bones) an inmate at Washington State Penitentiary. Bonz wrote well, and always with a bite, a rough edge that wouldn't hesitate to take a hostage. As much as I wanted to be in love with Bonz—I mean I wanted him to replace the empty space inside my soul—he wasn't Mark.

Nearly two years passed before Mark and I exchanged another letter. By that time I wasn't sure where he was. Across the state there are more than twenty prison facilities. Inmates get transferred. In December of 1992 I made my best guess and mailed a Christmas card. The card was forwarded. Mark answered in January from Lincoln County telling me Jasmine had slept with a prison pal who got out; in fact she had slept with several of his friends. His marriage was falling apart. Alone in my kitchen, and absolutely ecstatic to hear from him, I jumped up and down, "He's back! Oh, he's back! He's back!" That reunion happened nearly twenty years ago.

અ અ અ અ અ અ અ અ અ અ

More recently Mark and I talked about the direction our lives have taken. I've been with my partner, Paul, for seven years. Two years ago Mark married Michelle, an activist for human rights who lives in the city and helps newly released prisoners get back on their feet. Mark and I talked about our decision, thirty years ago, not to marry. In a way that sounded protective he said he didn't want me mixed up in the dysfunctional fringe of prison life. I think he holds me close to his heart in a place different from wife or lover. He saves the letters I send and my simple colored pencil drawings. There's a regulation about how much stuff— papers, books, and photos—a prisoner is allowed to keep. When he has accumulated a thick stack of letters he mails them back to me. I know he holds onto a few things that have special meaning.

When he was recovering from his near-fatal suicide attempt it seemed pages filled with words were too much. His brain hadn't recovered. I penciled winter trees, pastel clouds and a moon. I wrote: *On Tuesday evening I could see the full moon through bare winter branches and the clouds were grey-blue and pink.* The winter tree drawing he kept for nearly five years before he returned it. That's what I mean when I say he holds me close to his heart. When the world that surrounds him feels chaotic, and people have attached personal and political agendas to his life, and he feels helpless and out of control, and his only answer is to numb the pain and confusion by getting shit-faced drunk, and he can't see the choices he made that put him in a desperate situation, and everything falls apart, and even when I don't know where he is or how or why he is in trouble, still, we remain connected. I'm connected to him at a soul level, connected to the person beneath the criminal behavior.

Early one October morning, soon after we began exchanging letters, I released a lock of Mark's hair as a symbolic gesture freedom. I released it in the big river that runs through this valley. He had suggested the river, "...or plant some of it in a wide open space, a place that doesn't recognize steel bars and guns and captivity." It was early morning when I set his hair free and autumn mist was rising without restraint. I sat on dry weeds near the bank. As tears filled my eyes I wrote until my fingers were cold, until ink wouldn't flow, and until I couldn't think of anything more to say.

Today I walked down to that same river. It's January. The frozen river is covered with fresh snow and there are tracks: deer, raccoon, rabbit, bicycle, dog and boot. Although there's evidence of people passing through no one ever showed me how to find this place; I discovered it on my own. It was different thirty years ago, more secluded before they built the levee for flood protection and changed the course of the water. A hidden bird rustles in the tall, dry grass. Red willows reach for the sky and White Mountain looms in the distance. As I gaze in silence at the mountain I remember that day in October. I told Mark someday we'd come back to this place and I'd show him the river and the mountain. That was thirty-three years ago. I've come to this place many times but we've never come here together.

Intensive Supervised Parole

In April of 1998 Mark was released to a halfway house, more specifically a community corrections program in the city. Although he had the appearance of being free in the community his status with the Department of Corrections remained that of an inmate.

To simplify written language I have used the

word "parole" but Mark was on Intensive Supervised Parole, known as ISP, which means he had more restrictions and requirements than people on regular parole. In a backpack he carried an eight pound monitor everywhere he went, a modern day ball and chain. This device, along with the required ankle bracelet, tracked his movement 24-hours a day.

One morning I was in the bathroom watching Mark dry off after a shower. He put his right foot on the toilet seat; it was the first good look I'd ever had at the ankle monitor. It was a rigid black plastic case almost the size of a pack of cigarettes held in place by a one inch band of black plastic. As he toweled underneath the plastic case, I could see his skin was chafed raw from abrasion. He looked me in the eye, "Yes. It hurts. But it's better than prison." He had been living for three years by rules imposed by the Department of Corrections. At that moment I didn't think I could ever go through the humiliations that he was enduring for his limited freedom.

Mark had to get permission each time he left the halfway house. He had to sign out and he had to sign in. He had to obey the Rules of Association which meant no contact with anyone who had a criminal record. The irony of this rule is that everyone in the facility where he lived, all his peers, had criminal records. He was expected to build a new life without any of the people from his old life, the ones who stood with him

on common ground. When I think of all the requirements and the restrictions placed upon a parolee who
is building a new life outside the walls, I can't help but
think of indentured servants who came from Europe
to Colonial America. Passage on a ship was usually
arranged for a teenager by the father who signed his son
or daughter into servitude. The father worked out an
arrangement with a ship captain who didn't charge for
the journey across the ocean. The captain transported
the indentured servants to the American colonies and
then sold their legal papers to someone who needed
workers. Young men and women labored for a period
of three to seven years on a farm or for a merchant to
pay off their debt. They earned room, board, clothing
and training but were not paid for their labor. At the
end of the indenture the young person was given a new
suit of clothes and was free to leave. The assumption
was that the young person had learned marketable
skills and therefore had opportunities. Being forced
to leave everyone and everything behind to start a
new life, no matter how promising, is an arduous task.
Many indentured servants died before the end of their
servitude. Like indentured servants, parolees come to
a new world, the foreign world outside prison walls. A
parolee leaves prison with a set of street clothes, a check
for one hundred dollars, and then must face a harsh and
unforgiving world.

Mark met weekly with his parole officer. He

paid for being a resident at the halfway house and for the required counseling. He paid for breath analysis which was required four times per week; and urinalysis (UAs) four times monthly. After his move from the halfway house to an apartment there were random home visits from his parole officer. Any unexplained absence from the location where he was expected to be was called Out of Area and could levy the charge of escape, a reason to be sent back to prison. Having an unapproved visitor in his apartment was a parole violation. I know Mark's life of oppressive rules and few privileges was far more complex than what I've said here, and he faired better than most. Court fees and fines are frequently imposed and the wages of a parolee can be garnished to pay child support. Most parolees can never earn enough to support themselves and pay back the system.

After Mark's release to a halfway house his search for employment took a year. The question, "Have you ever been convicted of a felony?" is on job applications. Saying "no" is a lie that can cause a parolee more trouble, and responding "yes" means your application probably won't be considered. I feel outraged just writing about this legalized discrimination. The felon on parole is required to find employment and it's legal for all employers to discriminate against him. It is also legal for a landlord to discriminate against a felon. Felons on parole are not allowed to vote and they aren't eligible for government assistance programs; this includes food stamps. Against the odds Mark found a decent job working for a non-profit organization that raised money for environmental and social justice causes.

I remember talking with Mark on the phone one morning. He'd been employed for a few months and he wanted me to come downtown and see his new office. Since I didn't get to the city very often I had planned to go shopping. I was also hesitant about the situation with Barbie, his redheaded girlfriend from prison days. Their relationship was tumultuous. They were still involved and she resented me. He was trying to break free from her claws but she had deep connections with his sister and with his money. Barbie's identity as an activist was invested in Mark's successful transition from prison to the streets. Nevertheless, Mark told me how to find the building. At the end of the phone conversation I said, "Maybe."

That afternoon, after shopping for things I couldn't find, I found parking across the street from the office and watched as he strolled across the lawn. He was waiting for me. No longer that lean, muscle bound convict I fell in love with, he'd gained weight after hitting the streets.

He showed me around his new workplace, the call room he supervised and the bathroom down the hall. From the atrium I looked up to see six stories of offices above his. He wasn't allowed to go upstairs because it took him out of monitor range—that's the electronic device strapped to his ankle that tracked his location. I wandered up and down exploring the new surroundings.

Mark's garden level office had a college dorm look, social justice posters and lots of live house plants, all things he'd brought to give the place a homey feel. I liked what he had created; it was classy-funk. We talked. He liked his new job. Indeed, he was right at home hiring disenfranchised people from the half-way house and giving opportunities to street people.

Then he reached toward a shelf and put on a brimmed leather hat, like something from Woodstock. I looked at him and slowly shook my head. It was so out of place. The hat looked like something from a hippie-peace-love dream of what we would have been, if we had met in the free world, but we hadn't.

A call came in and it sounded like Mark was talking to his supervisor. "No, I cancelled the shift today. A bunch of callers called in sick."

Today's shift cancelled? Because I was there? I wondered but didn't ask.

"I knew you'd be here," he said to me. Words spoken like a mystic. *But how did he know I'd be here? I didn't even know I'd be here.*

"Something important is going to happen this afternoon. It's important. Whatever it is, whatever happens, it doesn't matter, it's important." That's how the seduction began—the seduction that started in a swivel chair and eventually took us to the floor.

Although there was plenty to resist in that moment, and I could have said "no" and walked out, this was, sort of, the opportunity we'd dreamed of for twenty years. Another one probably wouldn't come along anytime soon. *Why would I close this door? If I said no would I risk losing the relationship?* It was one of those ambiguous moments where I knew saying no would cause me as much turmoil as saying yes. I stayed.

There was no comfort on the thinly carpeted cement floor. I wasn't exactly submissive in that naked moment, I was angry. I reached my fingernails under his shirt and raked red scratch marks down his back leaving a message that would catch Barbie's attention and cause a hassle for Mark. With aerosol spray Mark made sure no odor lingered in the air and he tried to remove the stain on the carpet with paper towels.

It was time for me to leave. Barbie would arrive soon with Mark's ride back to the half-way house. Our twenty-year dream had been warm and sensual, but the actual experience was prison-like. Cold and hard.

Later that same evening at a restaurant across town college friends gathered for a reunion and I presented an award to our much-loved favorite history teacher. There's a picture of me with a brilliant smile standing next to my professor—inside I felt the shrapnel of betrayal as if a landmine had exploded.

If I had to describe my feelings in that moment—

that cold moment after I left red scratch marks down Mark's back, after he cleared the air with aerosol sol spray—well I couldn't. It was like the time I was in the women's locker room drying myself after a swim. My gold ring caught on my big toe nail and pulled the nail away from my skin. I let out an uninhibited yelp. A startled woman standing next to me gasped, "What happened?" Pain ripped through my body as I tried to soothe myself by applying pressure with my thumb to my toe. In that moment of intense pain I had no ability to speak. In that moment of intense pain with Mark I had no ability to speak and since I had gone along willingly I believed I had no right to complain about the abuse. In my mind an unmerciful voice of power and authority spoke, "You put yourself in that situation." Now I begin to realize that I have remained silent about sexual abuse for decades because I felt I had no right to speak. My relationship with Mark represents only a portion of the abuse. Only recently have I begun to consider that sexual abuse, even if I knowingly walk into it, and participate in it, is still abuse. This new way of thinking allows compassion to enter my wounded soul and allows love a place to begin its healing work.

かかかかかかかかか

Mark was on parole and coming to the end of his tumultuous relationship with redheaded Barbie when he met Julie, a professional woman in the office building next door. Mark invited me to meet her; he was certain I would like her. We met on a summer morning standing in the shade outside Mark's office. Julie had the energy of youth and sunshine, vibrant, well-educated, strong and practical. I liked her, but I was also envious. She was doing what I had longed to do for decades—helping Mark transition into the world: using real money, having encounters with self-service soda dispensers, learning the bus routes, finding his way through the grocery store and using electronic scanners. There were a lot of details to figure out. For twenty years I'd dreamed of transitioning with Mark; Julie had met him only a few months ago and got the job. Ouch! That rejection hurt. But I didn't show my anger and disappointment. I knew I couldn't live in the city. Although I silently grieved my loss, I also recognized that Julie was good for Mark.

Julie lived in the suburbs, she had a home with a yard—grass, trees, shrubs and flowers that needed attention. Mark was her self-appointed gardener. He spent Sundays at her home. I knew his Sunday afternoons with Julie included activities other than gardening.

One day Mark e-mailed a picture that Julie took in the park. Mark was eating French fries from a red McDonald's carton, the gold dome of the state capitol building shining in the background. It was the first picture I had seen of Mark in his freedom and I wasn't there. Julie was. I memorized every detail in that picture allowing the lonely feelings to echo through me. As I write these words the feeling of being left out washes over me again.

Mark's relationship with Julie reinforced that sense of betrayal. In those letters from prison Mark and I had painted a dream of our future. The dream gave us hope through many difficult years but the dream couldn't survive in the present. It is difficult to write much more without feeling the judgment again.

"I could've told you it wouldn't work," a friend once said to me. Then he laughed. I felt stupid and shut down. I tunneled inside myself to that place of worth-lessness. There was nothing more to say. From that place of worthlessness, I couldn't speak of how beautiful the dream had been, how we had nourished and sustained each other with hope. We could not have arrived on the outside in this new place of freedom without the dream that had kept us alive. The dream made the journey possible. But I've learned that not speaking is a way to protect my inner self from the pain of judgment. A story never spoken is a story that can't be judged.

People in general have a cocktail party curiosity about prison that goes as far as, "What's he in for?" and, "When's he getting out?" Those were the most frequently asked questions, but the ensuing discussion always seemed shallow and left me feeling agitated and empty. In time I quit mentioning that I had a friend in prison because I couldn't find the depth and truth of what really needed to be said about the love and the barriers.

What's he in for? As if a man is defined only by his crime.

When is he getting out? As if life doesn't begin until he arrives in the outside world.

The kindest attitude I ever encountered came from a hitchhiker I picked up named Leo. He only asked, "How long has he been down?" Those were words of compassion from someone who'd been down that road. Words of understanding that opened a door to discussion rather than shutting it by asking for the label of a crime and a date in the distant future.

Three years into Mark's parole I badgered him for more attention. He e-mailed saying that the events of our days were irrelevant. My heart sank. Why had the foundation of our relationship suddenly become irrelevant? But I knew his situation. I told myself that he was living on the edge with marginalized people, a fast-paced city life separate from my world. I realize now that at that moment I abandoned myself. When I gave him my understanding I denied and suppressed my own feelings. Refusing to accept his rejection I continued to write letters. I made my own envelopes cut and glued from the colorful slick pages of calendars: lilacs, forests, waterfalls, sunsets, and oceans. Handmade envelopes like these would have been rejected by the mail room when he was in prison. Even if he didn't read my letters his girlfriend Julie, who brought in the mail, would know that I was writing. It was my silent way of saying that I was part of his life.

Parole Board Hearing

I remember how much I wanted to be at the Parole Board Hearing. I was glad to be there. It was June of 1999 and I'd been a part of Mark's life behind bars for twenty years. Now the parole hearing, held at a downtown police station, marked a formal emergence into the world, a stamp of approval from the state.

With his neatly groomed beard and fresh haircut, Mark looked sharp. He wore a grey pinstriped suit, tailor made to fit. A mauve shirt and coordinating necktie brought the colors together like a picture from *Men's Fashion.*

While waiting for the formal proceeding I was introduced to Mark's supporters. It was odd how the names repeated; two men named Bob, two men named Bill, and two women named Mary. People who had loved ones in prison and long-time criminal justice reform advocates were Mark's allies. In recent months he'd corralled an impressive number of supporters from the metropolitan area. I was the only one who came from a long distance to be in a room of strangers with this one person I knew well, Mark Thompson.

Prior to the public hearing, the victim's family made their statement before a judge in a sequestered room. Mark had employment and was wearing the required ankle monitor, but the victim's family opposed him earning more freedom in the community—that's what I heard through a mutual acquaintance. Friends and supporters of the perpetrator weren't allowed to attend the private proceeding.

The public hearing took place in the largest room available which wasn't quite large enough for thirty-some advocates seated on folding chairs crammed together lining the cinder block walls.

After everyone was seated in the cramped room for Mark's public hearing, and the tape was recording, parole department representatives asked cold, official questions. They asked about the 1977 murder, about his ability to earn money, care for himself and lead a responsible life. Mark answered each question in a low, quiet and controlled voice. To show his compassion, redheaded Barbie, Mark's girlfriend, read a tearjerker statement about the sorrow and anguish Mark felt when he first learned about the Columbine school shootings. Although her wording was awkward, the sensitive portrayal of his reaction rang true to the Mark I knew.

A man from the parole board asked if there were additional comments but no one else volunteered to speak. The hearing concluded. Under the supervision of a parole officer, and with the portable tracking device,

Mark was allowed to continue living and working in the city.

The large group filed out of the small room. It felt like the end of a somber religious ceremony. People who knew each other formed chatty clusters and made plans to go to lunch or return to work. In this moment I needed to be comforted. I wanted a friend. I wanted to talk about what we had just witnessed in the hearing, to be a part of the advocates and supporters who knew each other. I imagined they would have included me if I had been able to reach out to them—but I was isolated by my own introversion and the power of this strange yet formal situation.

Mark was surrounded by an impenetrable circle of parole officials ready to usher him back to Community Corrections. As I headed for the stairs I caught his eye. He spoke out, "Give me a call tonight." I nodded. Then I listened to my footsteps descending the metal stairwell, echoing the emptiness I felt.

Mid-day traffic was heavy and I was in a section of town I didn't know. I planned to spend a couple nights at my parents' home in the city but I wasn't ready to go there. I knew that talking about the hearing would be disturbing to my mother. The subject was best left unspoken. If I had chosen an ordinary life—if I had married the appearance of financial security in the form of a doctor, a lawyer or a college president—I might have made her life easier. But I didn't, I fell in love with a writer who was in prison for murder and the emotional discomfort caused by my involvement, like all feelings in my home, was best left unspoken.

After the hearing it might have been nice to have ended up sitting on a park bench near a lake, or at that European coffee shop with lion statues by the door, but the place I found was a run down convenience store. I was still dressed up from the hearing in a white blouse and khaki skirt wearing nylons and my good leather shoes. I also wore the hand beaded necklace with matching rainbow colored earrings that Mark sent years ago as a gift from prison. In memory of prison visits I bought myself a cold diet Pepsi—that's what Mark and I always drank. I sat alone at the only table near a window where dust and flies had accumulated on the sill. I felt exhausted. The radio was loud and putting out more static than music. The table veneer was sticky, pockmarked and scratched with initials. The store smelled like rancid grease and hotdogs. A distracted customer bumped into my table causing my Pepsi to splash. He made no apology. I stared into space beyond this claustrophobic reality as customers outside filled their gas tanks. The twenty-year dream of getting out of prison had come true. Now the barriers were more complex. Mark's old girlfriend Barbie and his new girlfriend Julie each had their own relationship agenda with him. The case managers, the halfway house supervisor, and state correction officials all had a stake in Mark's success or failure. The officials who held positions of power didn't even know or care that I existed.

I once attended a memorial service for a close friend who committed suicide. The service felt very different from a service for an elderly person who died of natural causes. People avoided talking about what really happened. In the aftermath of the suicide, not only at the memorial service but also in the community, it was difficult for me to get any real information. The experience was oddly isolating. That's how I felt after this hearing. Only now, as I write these words, do I begin to understand that I was isolated long before this hearing began.

Who would I be without Mark?

Consider being held hostage for a day. Not at gun point but manipulated by a set of circumstances that draws your participation like being trapped in a dream. I think that's the best way I can describe the situation that unfolded on the millennium, New Year's Day 2000.

From Mark's apartment I walked down the path toward no place in particular thinking over twenty years of hopes and dreams. We had exchanged thousands of letters. I can't begin to count the miles traveled or the number of visits to the "cement garden," that's what Mark called prison. Although our friendship endured, the reality of life outside prison walls didn't bring us together as was once the dream. I sat down on a flat rock near a stream. A plastic bottle caught between rocks bobbed in the shallow water and two ducks seemed not to notice the icy cold. Twenty years of prison visits came through me as if they happened yesterday. The memories were accompanied by matter-of-fact tears. Like it or not this is how it is. This is where we are. Once again I heard the voice of authority: "You have no right to complain, you put yourself in this situation." I allowed time to pass while Mark visited in his new apartment with his new friends, holding them in suspense with tough ex-con stories. They all thought he was soooo cool.

What does one do in a sixteen-hour day that's owned by the Department of Corrections? This apartment would be his home in the future, but tonight Mark had to be back at the halfway house by ten. He was restricted by ankle monitor and couldn't go beyond the building.

Needing something to do, my self-assigned project was to clean his oven. Dissolving more than a year of greasy baked grime left by the previous tenant took most of the morning. Then friends arrived and Mark unintentionally, or maybe intentionally, excluded me from the conversation.

Who is she? What's she doing here?

Mark's new friends looked at me, the stranger, but didn't ask.

That's when I took my walk down near the stream. I invited Susan, the only other woman, to join me and felt disappointed when she wasn't interested. She stayed with her friends and the captivating prison talk. In this circle the vibrant Julie was known as Mark's girlfriend and I was a curious piece of furniture from the past that didn't quite fit the new arrangement.

After his friends departed we tried to find things to do; we moved a framed print to a higher position, we surfed the Internet and we pretended to be interested in a game of pick-up-sticks left from Christmas. We kept our hands off each other. We did everything to avoid and deny our physical attraction, but it persisted.

It wouldn't be right; after all, he had a girlfriend. He was faithful. He was loyal. It wouldn't be right.

I was the girlfriend from the past—a quiet, patient witness to two decades of prison life. Old love letters with promises about our future were inconsequential in this moment. His new life came with new people and new dreams. What about my feelings? That is a question I never asked aloud.

As daylight faded my unspoken and conflicted feelings intensified. My respect for Mark's relationship with Julie kept me from telling Mark my heart was wrenched and aching. My insides were throbbing from emotion too long on hold. As a child I was taught to walk away when I felt hurt or angry. Walking away wasn't an option; I wasn't going to leave him stranded. I remained the silent missionary.

I found more things with which to busy myself. Naturally inclined to domestic chores I couldn't resist folding the laundry. When I found her pink panties I ignored my sudden heart-sink feeling and folded them as if the owner were unknown.

Late in the day, after dark, after that silly attempt at pick-up-sticks, he could no longer deny the hard physical reality of our attraction. Mark and I both agreed what happened next would remain behind closed doors, but I will tell the reader the interaction was matter-of-fact, more about biological function than sensual play. He had to be back at ten; I gave him a ride.

When I think back on that day I see myself held hostage by my inability to speak my feelings. If I had spoken my feelings I might have woken from the dream. I might have discovered Mark didn't need me in his life. If that had been the case where would I go? What would I do with my emptiness? Who would I be?

I also began to see the pattern in our relationship: the longing to see each other, the intensity when we were together created by limits, and then the barrier of forced separation. Always the barrier.

Mark and Julie were still seeing each other and Julie was kind to include me when she knew I was coming to the city. She knew my history with Mark and encouraged us to spend a few hours together. I met Mark at his downtown office. There were papers he had to deliver across town. Rust, orange and gold leaves crushed beneath our feet as we walked toward Broad Street. Without a single spoken word, as soon as we were out of Julie's sight, we naturally reached for each other's hand. At the city bus terminal we stopped for a break. When Mark came out of the restroom I could smell the alcohol on his breath but didn't take it, consciously, into account. I'd arranged my life to be here, to visit Mark on this day. I didn't get to the city often and I wasn't walking away, aborting my plan. We boarded the shuttle and when it reached the end of the route Mark didn't stand up. The driver called, "last stop", and when we didn't exit he closed the doors. Suddenly, each minute was passing in slow motion. I wanted out. Mark was thinking about something. Maybe, *What can we get away with in the back of the trolley?* I wasn't exactly scared but this didn't seem like a good situation, me with a drunk convict on parole. I sat with him and I coaxed him. I wasn't going to abandon him and I couldn't move forward until he moved forward. Finally, he stood up and called the driver to open the doors. I breathed a sigh of relief as we stepped into the cool November air and walked a couple more blocks.

At the second office things didn't go any easier. Mark delivered the papers and flamboyantly flirted with the women asking, "Where's the coffee?" And when it was delivered he called out, "Edie! I love you, will you marry me?" Rage erupted in my veins. I'd had that love and marriage conversation with Mark too many times. We decided not to marry a long time ago, but that decision didn't mean I had no feelings—quite the opposite. Now he was recklessly tossing the idea of diamonds, satin and romance in front of an office acquaintance. A sick hurt feeling consumed me, like it had that time at the dance when my best friend flirted intensely with my boyfriend while I watched, but this was not the time to talk about feelings. I swallowed mine. Office interactions lasted until the women grew tired of his flirting and our journey continued down the elevator and out the front door.

A few steps outside the building Mark turned toward me and pushed his body against mine, pushed my back against the brick wall with a forceful and unforgettable hard, deep kiss—passion mixed with power and control in a public place. Sensual fear raced though me. I can only guess what was going on for him in that moment, but I wasn't enticed by the idea of drunken lewdness in the street. I urged him on down the sidewalk. We waited on a corner and caught the next trolley back to Broad Street. I stopped to use a pay phone; it was almost dark and I needed to tell a friend I was running late. Mark stood close by adding remarks to the conversation. "What? No, 'I love you'?" he asked, as I hung up the phone. He was in my face and I was completely annoyed and exhausted. "It wasn't an 'I love you' call," I snapped under the weight of accumulated irritations.

At the intersection we waited for the light, crossed six lanes of rush hour traffic and dodged a swift turning car. Mark adopted a softer mood, whispering promises. "Listen. There will be nights. There will be a time for us . . ." He waited with me until my bus came. I didn't know when I would see him again. That was the nature of our relationship—intense moments followed by long gaps of time. As I boarded the crowded city bus I released a big sigh. I felt safe and relieved to be leaving his drunken lewdness.

As much as I care about Mark, I can't control his behavior and it's best to be at a safe distance from a potentially dangerous situation. Again I hear the voice of judgment and condemnation as I write this story. "You never should have been with him in the first place." But get real. I *was* with him. Abruptly abandoning Mark in the city would have left me feeling far worse than walking with him on that afternoon—so I walked. I stayed with him. I've heard that I have the codependent behavior of needing to be needed—that I'm just as sick as he is. That we feed on each other. Sometimes the voices of judgment get so loud I try to escape by tunneling into the place of worthlessness but that's like trying to find comfort inside a red ant hill. The voices of judgment still haunt me but they are fading as I find better ways to deal with my own weaknesses and accept that Mark is capable of controlling his own destiny.

There was another incident with alcohol. It's yet one more moment that is easy for me to sweep under the rug and forget, but I can no longer deny that these things happened. They are part of my journey with Mark. These stories are difficult to share because I want to cover for Mark, and I realize as I write that I've been protecting him for a long time by not speaking. I don't want to admit that alcohol is a problem. He's my friend.

Mark was living in the apartment on Omaha Street so it was about three years into his parole. I was driving across town when he asked me to pull into a strip mall with a liquor store. I parked. He pulled out a fifty dollar bill and asked if I'd go inside and buy a bottle of something; maybe it was Scotch. I responded with numbed disbelief. *Am I supposed to do this?* If there were a guide book that goes with a convict on parole I'd never seen it, never read the written rules. I was the illicit girlfriend from out of town and the powers of authority directing Mark's life didn't know I existed. I sat in silence for a few moments. Quietly resistant, I asked some kind of question like, "Are you allowed to do this?" He put the money back in his wallet. I started my car and we went on down the road.

Come spend the night with me . . .

His timing. My timing. Our timing. Seems we never found harmony but that didn't stop us from trying. Accepting that things weren't going to work for Mark and me happened in bits and pieces, it happened circles and layers. In some respects it was like coming to terms with divorce. We'd have conversations about how and why our relationship wouldn't work and then try to make things work despite the obvious difficulties and barriers.

When I first met his girlfriend, Julie, she had explained that her relationship with Mark wasn't serious or permanent. But "not serious" is defined in so many unknown, hazardous and subtle tones, I knew to keep my distance. I knew "not serious" included sex, and "not serious" sex can be dangerous sex. I finally accepted, or at least recognized, that Mark and Julie were involved and their intimate relationship didn't include me.

At a weekend retreat in the mountains I met Jack. He was friendly and outgoing, and we shared a mutual interest in art and photography. He took an interest in me and I had a vacant spot inside that easily opened to a new relationship. We had been seeing each other for a few months when Mark decided to get in touch. I hadn't foreseen the chain of events falling into place, but Jack was the catalyst Mark needed to finally invite me to his apartment for a weekend.

My first response was, "I can't."

But I knowingly allowed myself to be charmed and lured. My second response was, "I have to tell Jack."

Mark said, "That can wait. You don't have to tell him now."

The discussion marked a very clear dividing line between Mark's values and mine. It wasn't the first time we had encountered different beliefs and standards, but this time I heard it in a new way because I was forced to make a decision. My girlfriend said, "If it were me I would go straight to Mark's arms and never tell Jack anything. You're not married. Jack doesn't need to know."

I was raised with a different set of values that made it hard to deceive anyone, especially when risk was involved, and sex always involves risks: broken hearts, sexually transmitted diseases, and pregnancy. Even when precautions are taken the risks remain.

If not now then when do I tell?

"If we are getting together, I have to tell Jack," so I did. I wrote a letter. No matter how gently I phrased it I knew the news was not good. Perhaps writing was unkind, but Jack lived two hundred miles away and he always seemed distracted and preoccupied during phone calls. I did what I thought I had to do in the murky waters of free love and uncommitted relationships.

How do I write about my first night with Mark?

Really, it began with lunch at the deli. He kept eating those yellow banana peppers. I don't know how many he ate, but he asked the clerk for extra and received a full condiment cup.

That evening, after his work, we rode the bus through the city. It was an hour and a half ride; we had to change busses three times. Being from a small town and visiting the city with romance on my mind, the long ride and conversation was a fun adventure, but he had to ride the bus daily. The daily ride was an absolutely grueling routine. By the time we got to his apartment the summer sun was going down.

Mark had a two bedroom unit on the second floor of a relatively new brown brick building. From his balcony he had a spectacular view of the parking lot. He didn't have a bed—he had a mattress on the floor. This was our first night together and he was very, very sick. Banana pepper sick. There was no sex. I felt disappointed, but forgiveness in this situation came easily. It's my pacifist upbringing. I've learned to replace disappointment with acceptance so quickly that I barely notice my sadness. That's how I moved through the naked hours of our night together. "It's okay. I understand." I snuggled close and he groaned from the agony of fiery spice.

As I drifted in and out of a dreamlike state, I remembered a clear vision of Convict Hill, the cemetery with a view of the prison, a place I often visited. I saw the circle of life and death, the circle of our relationship. Convict Hill overlooks the place where we began and is the place where we will end. Mark and I talked about that once, having our ashes scattered on the hill. I wrote the request in my will but he never put his in writing. And that—me being clear and precise, and him leaving his ashes to the winds of fate—reflects our eternal differences.

In the barely awake hours of early morning, I expected affection. I wanted him to hold me close, but he didn't. He got up to start the coffee as if my presence didn't matter. That bothered me more than his banana pepper episode.

I've thought about it a lot since that night together. I've thought about our relationship, my personality combined with his personality, and his prison sentence for murder. There's something in Mark's character that prevents him from being intimate in his relationships with people and I can't help but wonder if the passion in the murder that happened thirty-three years ago might hold this missing piece. It's taken me a long time to see this because in the beginning, deep trust and intimacy flowed through our letters, so I believed I would find intimacy in Mark when he got out of prison, but it wasn't there. It is true that we have a close relationship. We know how to make each other laugh and we have respect that keeps us from intention-ally pushing each other's buttons—yet we know where those hurt and angry places are. But there's a deeper level of vulnerability and trust that Mark isn't able to reach. There were emotional barriers that prevented him from being present with me. Still, when I order a deli sandwich I always ask for a few slices of banana pepper because it reminds me of that night together.

ৡ ৡ ৡ ৡ ৡ ৡ ৡ ৡ ৡ

On a Monday morning in August I gave Mark a ride to work, then spent the day cleaning his apartment. It wasn't anything I *had* to do; it was something I offered to do. He worked twelve and fourteen hour shifts and needed help. After two decades inside a cement box I was grateful he had a real place of his own. This cleaning was a celebration. With intense energy I went at it for hours: washed several loads of clothing, did the dishes, polished the mirrors, put fresh sheets on the bed, organized clutter into neat piles, scrubbed the glue-like tomato splatters inside the microwave, and the putrid grunge from the toilet. When I finished I took a long satisfied last look at the chaos that was now neat and organized. I left the key on his table and locked the door.

It was rush hour in the city. I was exhausted. Rain was falling. I struck every damn pothole in the road. Then, as I headed uphill, the traffic light turned red. I stopped. In that moment, in my exhaustion, in the rain, frazzled by traffic and jolted by the road . . . *This isn't working.* Mark needs a girlfriend and she, who ever she is, isn't me. He lives in the city, I don't. It was that simple and that clear. I couldn't hold on to the dream of our future any longer. Something had to shift.

What was I trying to hold on to anyway? The dream that I was his only ally? That I could rescue him from himself? A dream of happily ever after? A dream of being the one he loved?

Years ago I left this city and built a life for myself in a rural mountain community. I had held tight to the dream of *maybe someday* but on this day I knew for certain I couldn't live in this city with him and maintain my stability. I didn't fit into his post-prison lifestyle.

I returned to my rural home town where my work focused on organizing advocacy meetings. At one of the meetings I met a retired firefighter named Ken Smith. Ken was new to the area. He'd been kicked around by the system and took an active interest in my cause and the need for change in a human service system that wasn't humane. Together we interviewed marginalized people about their needs that weren't met by local agencies. We raised money by holding yard sales.

Our yard sales were always an event. Rainbow streamers floated from a tall sign that attracted yard "sailing" customers. Bluegrass music poured from a boom box, and cans of ice cold pop sold for fifty cents. This wasn't just a yard sale; it was a community gathering where people lingered and visited under the shade of an old elm tree. People came to support us by buying our stuff and by telling us their experiences of injustice.

It didn't take long before Ken and I developed a romantic relationship. Ken let me know he felt threatened by my two decade friendship with Mark. I decided it was time to make my commitment to Ken official. I needed to put a formal end to my relationship with Mark. Marriages have ceremonies and divorces should too. *I'm returning your stuff. Here. Take back the love you gave me.*

Ken was with me that day in June of 2002 when I went to visit Mark's office. I asked Mark to come outside and meet my friend. We stood in the asphalt parking lot. The visit was short, the time it took to smoke a cigarette plus a few minutes. To make it official I returned two keepsakes: a mirror etched with a unicorn beneath a rainbow that Mark had made in prison and a silver ring with a black onyx stone.

"Here!" I said in anger as I jammed the ring on his little finger.

Then, I reached into my bag and handed him the

mirror. Surprised to see it again after all these years, he thanked me and gently set it against a concrete parking barrier. He didn't yet fully understand that I was dissolving our relationship.

At the end of our meeting, when Mark reached down to pick up the mirror, I slugged him on the side of his head.

"Thanks a lot, Mary," he said as he stood up.

He was a convict on parole and in the middle of a work day. I'd never before hit him. I knew, given the circumstances, he wouldn't hit back.

It was a surprise attack. It wasn't fair. But things hadn't been fair for decades. Months earlier, in an e-mail, Mark had informed me he had yet another new girlfriend, Lisa. That was it. I'd had it. I was liberating myself from Mark's tangled web by returning two symbols of love from our relationship.

My hands were trembling and my knees were weak as Ken and I walked away.

In retrospect I doubt I ever would have slugged Mark if Ken hadn't been standing next to me. I slugged him to prove my new loyalty to Ken. Ken later complemented me on my courage but I didn't feel good about the incident.

It's so out of character—for me to hit anyone—it's rather hard to believe. I wouldn't confess to it here except to leave it out would be dishonest to the story.

My relationship with Ken lasted two years,

more or less. After he began receiving a disability check he moved out of my house and into his own apartment. Soon after Ken and I parted he got into an abusive relationship with a new girlfriend who sent him to jail on a domestic violence charge, but that's a separate story.

After I returned the mirror and the ring, Mark and I didn't see each other again for two years. I sent an e-mail, maybe two, but didn't hear back. Then, on the one year anniversary of our second divorce, as I called it, I wrote. It was June and I described summer happenings, I asked about his work, and I told him that I missed him. I didn't even know if he had the same e-mail address, but he did. He responded, "The reason I haven't contacted you is because at our last meeting you hit me. I won't tolerate violence in my life, not a second time." He went on to say he hoped that he would never verbally or physically harm another human being in his life. His non-violent message felt abrasive and harsh. *Who said I would hit him a second time?* His words echoed the unforgiving lesson of prison: *I will hurt you because you hurt me.* His unsympathetic words also reflected the lessons taught in the anger management classes he was required to attend. I didn't write back and another year passed.

❧❧❧❧❧❧❧❧❧❧

The next time I saw Mark was a day filled with uncertainties. City driving makes me nervous. I didn't know where I would find parking. Didn't know if I could find Mark's new office. Didn't know if he would be there. Didn't know if he would want to see me.

I purchased flowers at a quaint shop near the university. I planned to spend ten dollars, but they were waiting for a new shipment and there wasn't much to choose from. The clerk was friendly and helpful. Suddenly, the price no longer mattered. What mattered was that they were beautiful. I spent my last twenty dollar bill on large lilies with bright pink centers and a bunch of lavender mums. It was a tall and unusual arrangement, filled out with ferns. A bouquet to say, *I'm sorry.*

I drove downtown, not sure how I would locate Mark's office on that hard-to-find short segment of a diagonal street. I parked at a distance and carried those flowers through quiet, gently drifting snow flakes for nearly a mile until I arrived at the chrome and mirrored high rise.

In the elevator I took a deep breath against all the unknowns in this moment, tried to steady my trembling spirit, and pushed the button for the third floor.

The door pinged open into the refinement of soft sage colored walls decorated with a spray of flowers, a glass partition, more mirrors, and two young men in a casual mood at the reception desk.

"You have a flower delivery?"

"For Mark Thompson," I answered as my mind flashed back on how it used to be: filling out a form, presenting my driver's license, standing in line, removing my shoes, passing through a metal detector, being patted down, and receiving a stamp of ultraviolet ink on the back of my left hand. No earrings, no spandex, no sleeveless tops, no short skirts, and a long wait between the time I arrived at the visitor's entrance and the time Mark appeared in the visiting room.

The young man led me to a cubicle where managers were discussing business. Mark emerged. He seemed surprised and happy to see me as I handed him the vase of flowers. It had been two years since our last visit. We walked past a room filled with employees cramped into tight spaces like passengers on an airplane. Heads turned our way and for a moment I felt like I was living a Hollywood romance.

Mark sat the flowers on his windowsill and began fast paced chatty talk. "How is your car?" "How are your parents?" "How long will you be here?" The topics seemed irrelevant. My body had arrived but my spirit hadn't. I was still assimilating the long walk through drifting flakes, crossing through uncertainties, and the strange new surroundings. Not to mention reliving the surreal journey through life that brought me to Mark's restricted freedom. Freedom that didn't feel free. The transition left my psyche feeling wobbly.

Making a place for us to visit in private, Mark decided it was time for a cigarette break. As the elevator descended I looked into his face, recalling the first time I saw him behind prison walls almost 25 years ago. Much had changed and at the same time little had changed. We've held on, shared deeply, let go, attempted to dissolve our relationship more than once, and then come around full circle, together again.

Avoiding the large revolving door we took a side exit and stood in a walkway protected from the snow. He lit a cigarette and talked about his cats, Beijing and Oreo. He entertained me with lively chatter about Grasshopper, the newest kitten. "She sleeps on my chest and paws at my face with her little sharp claws."

He asked what I had been doing, and when I started to talk about producing programming for community radio he seemed distracted and uninterested. My world didn't connect to his.

I took a deep breath and brought up the real reason for my visit: the incident two years ago when I hit him. His last e-mail said I was a violent person and implied that he never wanted to see me again. That was the message lingering in my mind that brought me to his office with flowers and an apology. Mark said, "I forgave you a long time ago." *If he forgave me a long time ago then why had it been two years since we last talked?*

Standing in front of Mark his professed forgiveness angered me. If forgiveness were a card in a deck, he'd held that card too long.

Trying to make this unexpected visit last as long as possible, he lit a second cigarette. The subject changed before I could put my feelings about forgiveness into words. He told me his father died last October. His sister Debra from Iowa came to visit and brought some of his dad's clothes. Mark was wearing one of the shirts. "I had a Cadillac," he said. "It broke." That's all he said. The conversation skipped like a stone across water—skimming the surface, but avoiding the depth of what really happened.

He mentioned Lisa, called her his ex-fiancé. From my perspective Lisa was the reason we hadn't talked for two years. Mark said they "broke up" but she was still living at his apartment; she had no place to go. Then he told me he brings home other women who spend the night. Lisa doesn't like it and can't do anything about it.

Here's where I stepped out of my own *wounded girlfriend* feelings into my social worker role. This was my dance with Mark. This was how and why our relationship survived for decades. I flipped the switch, distanced myself from my feelings and listened. I didn't speak of the anger and injustice I felt. I didn't say I'm jealous of Lisa, although I was. Instead I offered silent thoughts of compassion for Lisa. I could only begin to imagine how tortured this relationship must be for her. I know how tortured any woman can become when seduced into the Thompson Trap. Drawn toward his charismatic charm and then cut out. He plays with you like a cat plays with a dying mouse.

At the end of our two-cigarette (plus a few stolen minutes) visit there was a goodbye kiss. He leaned into me, pushed my back against the building, kissed me the way he used to kiss me—long and deep and hard—like he meant it. Kissed me the way he always kissed me at the end of a prison visit. In this fading moment we were transient lovers. Then, we parted.

His situation still felt more like prison than freedom. Our time together had been shorter than any prison visit. There were new barriers, new relationships with new responsibilities. He had to get back to work. Through it all I got what I came for, a confirmation that our friendship—fragmented and patched, broken then glued—was not completely dead and forgotten.

As I walked away I wondered how much longer he'd be able to hold on. I felt like Mark was dangling from a strand of fraying twine.

ぷぷぷぷぷぷぷぷぷ

Using my non-dominant hand to write journal entries is a technique I used every morning for many weeks to retrieve lost memories. During this time of left-handed journaling I lurched awake from a nightmare. I felt the rushing vibration down the back of my legs telling me to run and freeze at the same time. I woke in a panic. It jarred loose yet another memory from my psyche. I remembered that day in September 2004 when I learned Mark was in trouble. I was staying at my parent's home in the city. I was going to visit my sister and had a Greyhound ticket to leave for Tennessee the next day. That evening I received a phone call from the Elmwood Police Department. My heart stopped in my throat and my hands started trembling. The officer said he was doing a routine safety check. Ken Smith was staying at my home and the officer wanted to know if he had permission to be there. Yes, he was a friend staying with my permission. A few minutes later, after the police were gone, Ken called me back. He said the police showed up looking for Mark Thompson. That's when I knew something wasn't right. I didn't know what had happened but I knew he was in trouble. Exactly what is the prayer for someone in trouble with the law, someone perceived as a threat to public safety? I wasn't denying that the external world felt threatened by Mark, but I knew his kind and gentle quality, the other side of the danger. As the Greyhound pulled out of the city I closed my eyes trying to visualize his surroundings but the vision wouldn't come clear. Wherever he was, whatever the circumstance, I hoped that he was not cold, not wet, and not hungry—words stolen from a Willie Nelson song. It was the best mantra I could come up with.

The bus headed east on the Interstate across the

plains of Kansas, past fields of wheat, sunflowers, and an occasional windmill. The most noticeable passenger was a lean, well-pierced and tattooed young man who looked to be about fifteen years old. He wore a black leather vest over a black t-shirt, black patchwork pants carefully stitched with dental floss, a wide silver studded belt around his hips, and heavy lace up boots. It was the stiff black Mohawk rising nearly a foot above his scalp that got my attention. How many bottles and cans of what did it take to create that? We left the city at eleven in the morning. Eighteen hours later, when we reached St. Louis, Missouri, his Mohawk had flopped sideways. As I waited for my Nashville connection I watched him disappear into a bus bound for Chicago. I couldn't help but remember being fifteen and wanting to escape my conservative surroundings, wanting to run away with someone like him.

From a payphone in Nashville I called Julie, one of Mark's former girlfriends, the one most likely to have and to share information. "Drinking and driving," she told me; "a near fatal car wreck." His girlfriend Lisa was with him and she was injured, maybe a broken collar bone, Julie wasn't sure. He holed up for two days with Lisa at the Lamplighter Motel, then called an attorney and turned himself in. Information had been broadcast on the city news, but I missed it all.

"You aren't going to visit him again, are you?" Julie asked.

I was waiting for my next bus in a noisy, crowded depot and Mark wasn't in prison, at least not at the moment. Her question went straight to my heart, the place where I ride the waves and swim through the darkness with Mark. I had no answer about the future.

ৡ ৡ ৡ ৡ ৡ ৡ ৡ ৡ ৡ ৡ

Five years after the near fatal accident that sent him back to prison, Mark told me what had happened. By then our visits had come full circle. We were sitting at a table in the visiting room at Kiowa, the same visiting room where we first met three decades ago. The assigned window stations were gone and industrial carpet covered the cement floor dampening the echo as steel slammed against steel behind me. The visiting room was now open with tables and chairs somewhat like a restaurant dining room. Below each tabletop a vertical board touched the floor preventing an inmate from touching the feet of his visitor or vice versa.

"It was the one year anniversary of my father's death," Mark began. Mark had been drinking. He totaled his new pearl white Pontiac Grand Am when he ran into the side of a city bus. His girlfriend Lisa was with him. On impact the seat belt restraint severely bruised her right shoulder, but didn't break her collarbone. He didn't say anything more about her injuries. The metal rod under the accelerator pedal pushed through the rubber and then through Mark's foot. He suffered three broken ribs, a broken foot, and a broken hand.

A few days after the accident Mark failed to report from home detention—a parole violation. He and Lisa had gone to a motel room. Mark overdosed on pain killers: 58 Percocet and a handful or more of acetaminophen. He told me it was the acetaminophen that poisoned his liver, the cause of his near death. He was sick. Very, very sick, but not dead. His urine turned thick and black, like molasses. This must have been terrifying. Before he turned himself in, minutes must have felt like hours waiting in limbo, never reaching death, but Mark didn't say that. After thirty-six hours of an unsuccessful death attempt, Mark made the call to his parole officer and turned himself in.

City police, an entire SWAT team, and medical rescue swarmed the scene with flashing lights and sirens. Lots of cops. They surrounded the area. It was sort of like aiming a fire extinguisher at the flame of a lone birthday candle.

"Put your hands up!" "Surrender!"

Mark was sick, dying, and surrounded at gun point. An ambulance took him to City Hospital. In the emergency room they brought him back. Shocked his heart with the paddles. It was at this point he had a choice. He remembers the attendant telling him it was a choice, asking him if he wanted to live. He was nearly dead yet chained to a gurney to prevent his escape. He said he wanted to live. They shocked his heart a second time, brought him back to life.

The most profound thing Mark revealed during this visit was the deep sadness he felt when he was coming back from death. No white lights, no tunnels, no spirits like many people describe in near death experiences—but a profound sense of sadness. He knew he wasn't finished with this life.

Before the suicide attempt he had packed his personal belongings and labeled each box with the name of the intended recipient. He left behind written instructions, his last wishes. It was sort of a homemade last will and testament that wasn't notarized, wasn't official, and wasn't honored. After his suicide attempt, people from his office, people he once called friends, cleaned up his apartment and threw all his stuff into the dumpster including his dad's firefighter helmet.

Yes. Including his dad's firefighter helmet. We both lament the loss of the helmet. The one with the name Thompson lettered across the back. The one his dad wore during his forty-year fire and rescue career. The helmet that bore witness to the strength, hope, and life his dad gave to victims of emergency disasters. The same helmet Mark received in the mail after his father's death.

After being brought back to life at City Emergency, law enforcement took Mark to county jail and then the Reception and Diagnostic Center where he was processed back into the Department of Corrections.

It's a very long journey, coming back from near death.

For a long time Mark hated himself for being a failure at life and then for being a failure at death. He tried to soothe his injured psyche by overeating and he gained a lot of weight.

I knew he had gone back to prison, but I didn't know where. Prison in this state isn't one place; it's more than twenty facilities spread throughout the region. I addressed a letter to the place I thought most likely to house him and when the letter was returned I tried another. Don't know why it took me so long— probably because I hate dealing with bureaucracy—I finally remembered Inmate Locate. I accessed it through the Department of Corrections on the Internet. I found Mark at Crow Valley, a facility practically at the state line, 375 miles from my home. But I found him. I found him!

I knew the suicide attempt affected his brain function and thought processes, not to mention his overall physical health. When I wrote I sent simple pencil drawings and fewer words. Gradually, he lifted the veil from tragic events and allowed a few outside friends into his locked world. A year passed before I received a letter, then, three more. I often wondered but didn't know if we'd ever see each other again.

やややややややや

Built less than ten years ago, Crow Valley is the newest of more than twenty correctional facilities scattered throughout the state. It has a capacity to hold 2,450 men and employs 800 people in a remote area that some might call prairie wasteland. The description on the Internet reads, "The Department of Corrections strives to make visits *comfortable* and *pleasant*." No doubt the words comfortable and pleasant have many interpretations. Crow Valley has the strictest restroom protocol I've ever experienced. At 10:00 a.m. the guard barks "Restroom!" I'm the first one out of my seat as I needed a restroom break an hour ago. The women, maybe fifteen of us, line up against the cement wall. There are two separate sink and toilet rooms each with a solid door—not a row of six toilet stalls inside one long narrow room like a woman would find in many public places.

The female guard stood behind me and I knew to reach out in the form of a cross as she ran her hands up my arms and then down my back pausing to make sure my bra fastener wasn't concealing anything. I turned. She faced me and placed her hands on my shoulders, brought them forward like the letter V between my breasts slowing to make certain no foreign object was hidden in my bra. Next, "Pull out your pockets," the white fabric lining the front pockets of my jeans. Then,

"Open your mouth and lift your tongue." She looked inside with a little light. After I passed her search—the second search since I'd entered the facility—I was allowed to enter the toilet room. And after using the bathroom it was the same search one more time. A third search before I was allowed to return to the table in the visiting room. At other facilities, sometimes a female guard was tactful and somewhat polite about the required search, but not at Crow Valley. At Crow Valley I could feel the hostile power and control like a current of electricity keeping inmates and visitors in their place.

❧ ❧ ❧ ❧ ❧ ❧ ❧ ❧ ❧ ❧

It's a two and a half hour drive from the city to Crow Valley Correctional Facility on the eastern plains. The December morning was clear, below zero, and hoar frost glittered on bare branches. I rode with Mark's friend and soon to be wife, Michelle. As we headed into the rising sun, Michelle told me stories of successful lifers. The successful lifers were men who had served a life sentence—twenty years—and been released. She knew them through her years of advocacy work with newly released prisoners, helping men get the basics like food, clothing and a place to live. She had connections with a Lifer's Group that met monthly for mutual support. Michelle told me about the guys who were out on the speaking circuit telling their stories and giving hope to others. She didn't come out and say it, not exactly, but it seemed like this was the hope she held for Mark. It was the same dream for success that I once held.

At Crow Valley we tolerated the familiar check-in ritual: filling out a form, presenting drivers' license, removing shoes, passing through the metal detector, being patted down, and receiving a stamp of ultra violet ink on the back of the left hand. We walked down a long cement corridor and entered the visiting room. A guard assigned us to table number seven. Then, we waited for Mark to appear.

I'm not sure how to describe my reaction to his dramatically changed appearance. Over the past four years he had gained 80 pounds and his forehead was balding. Thin graying hair now down to the middle of his back reclaimed his hippie status. I must have been holding my breath, I realized, when I silently gasped. Maybe I reacted the way a mother reacts to a child who is seriously disfigured in an accident—she sees the dramatic external change but knows that inside the shell of a disfigured body the memories, life experiences and heart connection remain.

"How ya doin' Pal? How was your drive? It's good to see you." When I heard the familiar sound of his gentle and confident mid-western voice I felt comforted and I relaxed.

Aside from Mark's changed appearance, two things stand out from this visit. One was when I asked, "What do you see from your window?"

He paused for a moment then said, "From my window I see a fence, the kill fence, and beyond that another fence with a spiral of razor wire. Sometimes a rabbit. And after dark, a twinkling of lights from town." The description is perhaps ordinary but the fact that he could describe it—that's what has kept us together. When most men held for too long in captivity would have answered with a bleak, "Nothing. There's nothing to see," Mark could put words to the scene. It was a moment that reminded me of the man I fell in love with thirty years ago—he's good with words.

The second thing I remember is Michelle telling Mark she found out that George Davis was buried in the Prairie County Cemetery. *Why had I never thought to ask?* I mean, I've been involved with this murder story for three decades. Of course the victim has a story that needs to be heard. In that moment I was called by a force outside myself, call it a higher power if you will. Call it the evangelical influence of Sister Helen Prejean, the Roman Catholic nun who crusades against the death penalty. I knew that I needed to pay my respects to the other side of this story.

A few days later I went to the cemetery, found the grave and took pictures. Doesn't that sound easy? There's more to it. December 15th was my birthday and also the thirty-first anniversary of the murder.

As I looked at my reflection in the mirror my silent request on the morning of my fifty-third birthday was that I would find the grave of George Davis.

There was a festive family celebration that afternoon. My birthday party went on, and on, and on with a surprise visit from my partner Paul, dinner, cake, candles, ice cream, balloons, many gifts, and lots of pictures. It was a wonderful party but I wanted to find that grave before dark and we were pushing sunset. I mention this because it has always been a balancing act, keeping my friendship with Mark separate from my family—honoring the boundaries of love. My family prefers not to know the details of my involvement with a felon so I couldn't very well announce that I wanted to cut my party short so I could go to the cemetery because it was the anniversary of the murder.

On the Internet I found an address for the cemetery—let's just say it was easier to find on the Internet than it was to get there. Paul was with me. As the veil of dusk descended we took off in separate directions. There was a lot of ground to cover and I had no idea which way was right. About twenty minutes later, in the muddy fresh snow in the northeast corner of the cemetery, Paul called to me. He found the Davis site. Before I give my thoughts as an observer at the Davis grave I want to offer this story of murder in my family.

Murder in My Family

I wonder if there is a difference between the heartache, grief and suffering in a family abruptly abandoned and suddenly without a father after the violent act of murder, and the heartache, grief and suffering of a mother who learns her son has committed a brutal murder? In each case murder is an act that forever changes the shape of a family. It changed the shape of mine.

Nine years before I was born, a murder happened in my family. It's reported in the *New York Times*. My Great Grandmother Christine would have been 58 when she learned Richard, the third of her five children, killed someone on Staten Island. According to the *Times*, February 18, 1946, Ava and Lily Mercer, 80-year-old recluse twins, were found bludgeoned to death on the kitchen floor of their dilapidated nine-room dwelling in Staten Island. Richard was 32 at the time. He'd been drinking. He went to his cousins, the Mercer sisters, and asked for money to buy liquor. When Ava refused they quarreled. Richard picked up a stick of pine firewood and used it to bludgeon first Ava, and then Lily, when she tried to help her sister. An autopsy confirmed each woman died from a skull fracture. The newspaper report went on to say the sisters spent most of their time in the kitchen of their weathered, decaying home which was without electricity or gas. All the rooms except the kitchen were tightly shuttered. In an upper bedroom a dozen or more dollar bills were stuffed into the crevices of a window sash to keep out the cold and to stop the rattling of the panes.

That's the lore of the story that has been passed down, rumor of the sisters' wealth stashed inside a mattress. In the end confederate bills were found; it's said ancestors ran guns on the underground during the Civil War.

Richard did time for the murder at Sing Sing in upstate New York. I don't know any details about his trial. I heard he did six years and got out early for good behavior.

Richard was my Great Uncle. I remember meeting him only once when I was fifteen and visiting the Island with my Grandmother Grace. Richard would have been sixty. I was waiting in the car with my Great Aunt Louise and Grandma, sitting in a parking lot near the post office. In retrospect, Richard probably arranged to meet his sister Louise because she managed his social security check, but at the time I didn't know those details. I don't remember what we said; the interaction was brief. What I've always remembered is the feeling of Richard's kind and loving presence. I was sitting in the back seat, car door open to vent summer's heat. He knelt down eye level with me. He was genuinely pleased to meet me, Grace's granddaughter from Wyoming.

I imagine Richard had an undiagnosed bipolar

disorder and drank to self-medicate, at least that's the story I tell myself. As far as I know the demon of alcoholism was with him until his death. He had long periods of sobriety but never kicked the habit. "He was the kindest person you'd ever want to meet unless he was drunk," as my dad once described Uncle Richard.

The memories I have of my Great Grandmother Christine are few but vivid. Especially the time I was in her bedroom and she opened the cedar chest to show me a quilt, but what came out was the story of the red plaid flannel shirt. "That's Richard's Christmas present," she said to me. "Dianne wouldn't take it to him. It broke my heart." I was 15, Great Grandma was 83. I didn't know the details. Didn't know Dianne. Didn't know about the murder. Didn't know why anyone would refuse to help an elderly woman by delivering a Christmas gift. But whatever the circumstances Great Grandma's profound sadness made an imprint. I feel the sadness again as I write these words. It's as if she gave me a clue about the murder while never saying a word about what really happened.

Murder leaves holes in a family. In December of 2002 Jackie, a cousin in New Jersey I never met, e-mailed, "I am desperately trying to link with my family which has been a big void." Jackie went on to identify her father as Richard Mercer. Her mother was 15 when she married Richard and they divorced when Jackie was a toddler. "There's always been mystery surrounding the Mercer side of my family," she wrote.

A few days later Richard's granddaughter wrote, "Any information is greatly appreciated as we are very interested in knowing and passing on to the next generation family folklore and stories. I'm trying to research what happened with Richard." Initially, there was a flurry of e-mail as we, distant cousins, discovered a new connection and shared what we knew about family history, vague details of the murder, and our own daily lives. Whatever the reason—maybe because we didn't find enough common ground in our present day lives—we haven't stayed in touch. Murder changes the shape of a family.

When I called Ocean View cemetery I found out Richard is buried next to his mother. I imagine she, Christine Mercer, always grieved for her son. Always asked herself, "What could I have done differently?" Of her five children, he's the only one buried in the same cemetery as his parents.

When I think back on the summer I visited Staten Island I think maybe I represented hope to my Great Grandmother and to my Uncle Richard. Before I was born, my branch of the family had moved west, off the Island toward more opportunities, higher education, better jobs and a new way of life. I wasn't the only great grandchild, but I was the one who came from a different walk of life, a changed family environment. I was removed by nearly two thousand miles and two generations from the alcoholism that murdered two elderly cousins.

Looking back on the family dynamics I see the hope for a better life and a better world that ancestors place on youth. In the early seventies I was that spirit and symbol of youth for my family.

Just as my ancestors held the light of hope for me I have always held the light of hope for Mark. In the beginning it was the hope of a life together as activists for social change. Over the years the vision has changed, but not the hope I hold for his future, his recovery from alcoholism. He doesn't believe alcohol is a problem in his life. I believe it is—an unacknowledged demon that will strike again if he doesn't take the first step toward recovery. I can't do it for him but perhaps I can cast a light on the door.

❧ ❧ ❧ ❧ ❧ ❧ ❧ ❧ ❧

More than a year after Paul and I first located the Davis gravesite I returned for another visit. I carried a long screwdriver and a garden claw to loosen the dirt. I also carried silk flowers—half a dozen yellow roses—down the dirt and gravel road to the northeast corner of the cemetery. I hoped the soil would be moist, hoped that I could easily puncture a hole in the earth, push the plastic-wire stems into the ground and be done with it. But the ground was dry and rock hard. I stabbed it with the screwdriver for a long time. I stabbed at it as I remembered what I knew about the murder. George Davis was killed with a hunting knife that severed his aorta. I stabbed at the ground knowing that my lover was the last person who had seen Davis alive.

It was taking longer than I wanted, digging this hole above an unseen casket of decaying flesh and bones. I didn't know the family but I knew the story beneath the granite marker. I knew how Davis made his sudden involuntary exit from this world more than thirty years ago. I felt like I was trespassing with flowers into a private world filled with pain where maybe I didn't belong.

What is this about? What am I doing here?

These were the questions I asked myself. Sometimes when I'm in a quiet place I feel another presence and something comes through me, as if I am a vessel for some larger purpose—that's how it seemed when this message drifted in on silent wings: *Release the hatred that surrounds this crime.*

I continued working the hole, pulling the powdered dirt forward with my gloved fingers, until finally the hole was six inches deep, deep enough to support the tall stems. I planted the roses and packed the dusty dirt, then covered the scraped ground with long pine needles and scattered a few pinecones leaving the impression that the roses magically appeared. I couldn't undo what happened thirty years ago, couldn't wish George Davis back to life. If he hadn't died I never would have met Mark; the events of both my life and the Davis family would have been different. I was at the gravesite because I needed to acknowledge, within myself, what had happened. I needed to leave yellow roses, an unspoken token of respect and compassion for the family. Although we have never met, my life has been touched by their tragedy.

I was touched by the tragedy again when I visited Mark's new wife Michelle. She pulled out a box of pictures, some sent by Mark's sister Debra and others from mutual friends. A few black and white snapshots from the family home in Iowa, pictures of the growing up years, Watson the family dog, Christmas, and Mark's brief stint in the Navy. There were pictures of Mark's sister Debra, his mom and dad, and a few people I didn't recognize. Then, the girlfriend photos: soft glamour shots of Jasmine looking like a movie star, and pictures of redheaded Barbie acting silly with a giant sausage at a picnic. A third of the pictures in the box were ones I'd sent to Mark.

As I looked through this box of pictures with Michelle I thought the Davis family has pictures with memories, too—but I don't know how to represent their side of this story. I know the story of Mark's loss, a life spent in captivity, but aside from what I've read in the papers and my visit to the gravesite I don't know their personal story of loss. I like to think that if the Davis children, Daniel and Josephine, were to read this story that it might unearth the discovery of a common human bond that has the power to heal. The man who killed their father is human, suffering and afraid, just like they are.

Letting Go of the Outcome

In order to make sense of Mark's relationship with alcohol and my relationship with Mark, I've started attending a twelve-step recovery group. Years ago, when I first learned about it, the language of codependency didn't make any sense. The lines of the victim's triangle might have appeared clear when drawn on a chart but they weren't clear in real life where roles often shift and blur. The perpetrator-rescuer-victim dynamics can be played out by people, but the voices of the unseen perpetrator-rescuer-victim can also play out within myself. The perpetrator often appears in my own harsh and self-accusing judgments. Although I sometimes get lost in complicated explanations, I do understand that there is a pattern to the dysfunctional relationships and it's easier to define my own than it is to define Mark's.

Quoting from a book that was life-changing in my recovery from a severe eating disorder, "There is a tendency in anorexic families for each member to speak not for him or herself but in the name of another member, always modifying, correcting, or invalidating what the other person has said." Here's one example of speaking for someone: I'm wearing a purple shirt and my brother walks into the room. I know he hates the color purple. Rather than allowing him to have his own response when he sees me, I anticipate what he will say and I jump ahead. I respond with the words I think he will say. I say, "I hate purple."

In my family we frequently jumped ahead and anticipated what the other person would say, not allowing the individual to speak her own thoughts or reaction to a situation. In conversation, often before I finished speaking my thought, someone else would be projecting their ideas on top of my words and I, an introvert, retreated into myself for protection rather than fighting to be heard. Day-to-day communication that involves individual feelings, family activities, and family conflicts is more complex than simply the color of a shirt, and I found myself attempting to distill meaningful information from indirect and sometimes vague comments.

I learned to ask indirectly for the things I wanted, because a straight forward approach that included feelings was uncomfortable and threatening for me and for the person I was speaking to. In my family there was also a pattern of trying to rescue or save the other person from their own feelings—always trying to soothe, minimize or prevent the emotional pain of disappointment and other losses. This was a pattern of denial.

Sometimes, when I was older, I wanted to speak out of my silent oppression and say, "You misunderstood," or "Your assumption isn't true," but the conversation raced forward and I lacked the courage to speak out and contradict the power of authority. Then, when I felt unheard or misunderstood because I didn't speak out, I retreated into my own world where unspoken hateful thoughts, aimed at myself, circled like unrelenting vultures in my mind. This pattern, established long before I ever met Mark, is one place where my feelings of isolation and exclusion began to develop. I didn't understand this dysfunction and the resulting emptiness when I was growing up; it is the twelve-step recovery work that has helped me to understand and find a healthier way to interact and be present to people in the world.

In the story about a murder in my family that happened nine years before I was born I wrote, "I wasn't the only great grandchild, but I was the one who came from a different walk of life, a changed family environment. I was removed by nearly two thousand miles and two generations from the alcoholism that murdered two elderly cousins." But had my family really changed? Did time and distance remove us from the dysfunction? Or was the dysfunction inherited like I inherited the shape of my nose? Although there was neither active alcoholism nor substance abuse in my family, the dynamics and the perpetrator-rescuer-victim behavior described in the victim's triangle was present.

Friends in the twelve-step recovery program help me understand. They recognize the dynamics. Patterns like extreme self-sacrifice: adjusting to any situation no matter how terrible and never giving up, even when giving up or letting go is the choice that will allow natural consequences and will give everyone the freedom to move forward. Twelve-step friends understand absorbing injustice: taking responsibility for things that aren't my fault. Twelve-step friends remind me that kindness doesn't mean allowing others to take advantage of me. The pain of examining these behaviors, reading self-help books and attending recovery meetings is sometimes like walking barefoot across sharp gravel.

These behaviors, like indirect communication and rescuing others from their own feelings, have colored my internal landscape for more than fifty years. Finding a new point of balance doesn't come easily, but staying in the old place of denial and trying to indirectly control the behavior of others no longer works, either.

෴෴෴෴෴෴

In last night's dream I stood in a vacant lot looking at a nearly collapsed wooden fence. The yard was dark and eerie like Halloween with twisted trees, low hanging branches, and dry leaves caught in tall grass. As I stood there in silence the dark quiet yard came to life. Strange creatures like I have never seen began to emerge. A large dark bird with a pelican-like beak ran toward me, his wings flapping with the energy of a dog. The creature came toward me with force and then stopped. He made a barking-squawking noise but didn't attack. Other strange creatures awakened in the yard. One had four legs and long shabby hair covered its body but there was no visible head. They were surreal creatures from some exotic land, mythical dog-bird-people. This dark silent world was disturbed by my presence. When I woke I wrote the dream in my journal and then, my mind wanting to make sense of it, I wrote: "The silent dark yard is like the dark energy of the universe. I have disturbed the energy and it has come to life."

I can't help but feel I have disturbed dark, trapped energy by telling my story. I have brought into the light my sometimes strong and sometimes frail emotions that have been protected too long by introversion and shadows. By telling my story I've also crossed another bridge into the unknown, like the day I carried flowers to Mark's office not knowing if I would find him, not knowing how he would react.

Seven months after I began writing this story I got the news that Mark would be released on parole this summer. His parole came about with support from a network of people in the city, including the former District Attorney and Mark's wife Michelle. Mark's petition for commute made it to the governor's desk just weeks before the governor left office. It's a tradition for an outgoing governor to pardon or commute offenders when he believes the decision serves justice. An untold number of prisoners hang their legal hopes on the governor every year, but only a few receive his mercy. In Mark's case the injustice was called "disparity of sentencing." When he returned to prison on an escape charge that followed a parole violation—drinking and driving, the near-fatal car wreck, and the near-death suicide attempt—the court added twenty-three years to his sentence. This was a "disparity" because no other inmate in this state who returned to prison on an escape charge has ever received a setback as harsh as the one meted to Mark. He contested the sentencing law and won his case when the outgoing governor signed his commute.

I knew of the hope for this commute more than a year ago when Mark's supporters began compiling the documentation. I too wrote a letter of support to the Executive Clemency Board. And I sincerely wished Mark the best of luck. This time my support wasn't heavily laced with my dreams for a future together. Many times through the years I rode that wave of hope with Mark, the hope for one legal appeal and then another. The belief that he would be out by Thanksgiving, followed by the belief that he would be out before Christmas, followed by the crash of disappointment and deep despair when yet another appeal was denied. I didn't ride on this one. The outcome was not in my hands. When I received the phone message from Michelle saying that Mark would be paroled this summer, I gave a spontaneous victory shout like they do when someone scores at football. I was surprised by the news, but also glad for my distance from the wild energy and excitement among his supporters in the city. It's taken a long time to work through my feelings about Mark's relationships with other women, but I can honestly say I'm grateful this time that Michelle and Mark will have each other for support.

٭٭٭٭٭٭٭٭٭٭

It's a clear spring day and the sun gently warms my back. The trees have a feathery green haze that speaks of new life emerging and petals from apple blossoms drift. This is a time for new beginnings. I sit on the cement slab atop Convict Hill with a view of Kiowa Correctional Facility downhill and across the river, less than a mile away. My pen and journal are in hand although it's hard to know what to write, so I stare into the distance knowing where Mark and I have been, knowing that things are changing, and knowing that our paths—at least in this earth-bound existence—are separate. Through the years I've sat on this hill in all seasons, when the cement slab froze my rear end and when it scorched the seat of my pants. I've been here when the gravel hill sings with locusts, when the prickly pear cacti bloom, when October trees are crimson and orange, and when summer lightening cracks a grey-green sky.

Today when I climbed the hill I found the skin of a bull snake that disintegrated when I touched it. Native people say Snake is a sign of transformation—the cycle of life, death and rebirth. It fits. Mark will be going to the city to start a new life with his wife Michelle. I sense change coming into my life as well.

Mark knows that I'm writing this story. I've mailed him drafts and asked for his comments. I don't hear from him very often but when I do he tells me, "Mary, there's only one point of view. Yours!" I agree. This is my story told from my point of view. "I know your story is different from mine," I say. "And I hope you will write yours."   ৵

Hello My Baby,

I'm back again. Outside the sky has turned rough, and black clouds cover up the setting sun. The colors are beautiful; deep purples flowing against rose and gray. I wish you were here to see it through with me. Maybe it will actually rain.

Yes, I'm getting all of your stuff (I know how you worry about such things.). Then you said that you wanted me to know that you care. I know. Love is one thing---very wonderful and fulfilling in it's own right---but caring is something else entirely. I find myself intrigued by the amount of care we share. I do worry about you in your daily routine, and I know that you wonder what I'm doing at any given time. I've not painted a very pretty picture of life in here... I've given you plenty to worry about. I could get into all kinds of trouble, without even trying. But I don't. I have a goal to reach in my life and a woman to see me reach it. I'm not going to fuck up whatever small chance you and I have at finding happiness. You've become so much a part of my life that I automatically think of how my actions might effect the outcome of our relationship. That means that I love you one hell of a lot.

Letters from the Pen

12 Selections, 1980 – 2009

Letters from the Pen

Emerald, Gold and Rose
August 28, 1994

Prison Suicide
October 3, 1980

"90 Proof"
May 17, 1981

Killing a Rabbit
April 25, 1982

The Influence of Violence
June 1, 1982

Stop Kicking Us
May 8, 1988

The Catharsis of Writing
August 7, 1990

I Became a Person
August 6, 1994

Letter from Cactus County, Texas
August 8, 1996

Thoughts on 9/11
September 13, 2001

My Thoughts Fall into Holes
August 28, 2009

In Love
September 28, 1980

Emerald, Gold and Rose

Broken Arrow Correctional Facility
August 28, 1994

Dear Mary,
        I wonder what you are doing
right this moment. Earlier I took
time out to go see the summer shower
that blew in, stayed just long enough
to make deep puddles everywhere,
and then moved on. I went outside
a moment ago and saw a beautiful
rainbow. Just three colors, emerald,
gold and rose, but very distinct, very
beautiful, very moving. I'm just in
that kind of mood tonight. The clouds
were whiter than cotton and lingered,
almost as if they had been torn from
the belly of the storm and left behind
when it passed. They kind of lazily
hung in the air below the tops of the
mountains and quietly blew apart,
their stringers drifting half across
the sky. The mood was refreshing, and
I needed it. I know that I complain
a lot about work, but work is truly
grueling. I often don't leave the
office until eight at night, a very
full day. I drag in and shower,
trying to put everything back together
again and find some peace. But then I
live with someone, so peace is just

out of reach, always. It will be
nice to choose who I live with when I
finally get out.

[Excerpted from a longer letter and signed:]

Good Night My Love,
Mark

Prison Suicide

Kiowa Correctional Facility
October 3, 1980

Dear Mary,

A terrible thing happened last night, Mary. And I was a part of it. A boy, no older than 19 or 20, hanged himself in his cell. He cried for help in a hundred ways that day and no one listened. He was no more than a child really, a little boy, trying to live in a man's world. He didn't belong in this place. He was only doing 1 to 2 years. The boy belonged in a county jail, or on probation, but not thrown into a world he neither understood nor could cope with. They seem so much younger at 19 these days than they did when I was that age. Maybe it's my mortality catching up with me.

The boy's name was Smith, and he repeatedly asked for psychiatric help in adjusting. His pleas fell on deaf, uncaring ears; and so he wandered through his short time here as if in a dream world, sometimes stumbling, with no one to help him up.

The afternoon of his death he asked for help from the cell house officers, telling them that he would kill himself if they didn't send him to see the psychologist. They turned back to their work and ignored his interruption.

God, he was so small and helpless.

And then he sat down on the bench next to me and asked if he'd seen me somewhere before; that I looked familiar to him. He suggested that maybe he'd seen me in the federal joint or something. For the first time I really took a look at him. His wrists were bandaged from an earlier suicide attempt with razor blades and he looked so damn YOUNG. I looked at his number and saw that he was new and jumped to a conclusion I'll regret for a very, very long time. I thought he was a fish trying to make an impression on me and I decided to get rid of him as soon as I could. I told him that no, I didn't know him and that I'd never been to federal prison. I didn't see how he could have been either, being so damn young. I just shined him on, only half listening to him, not recognizing his hurt. I only wished he'd leave me alone with his sob story. I failed to see the pain and fatalistic wound in his eyes. Fuck, Mary, this is hard.

I HAVE let this place harden

me. I've let it sap all the surface Mark, what I thought was the real me, into an impenetrable shell. I didn't care; I didn't want to be bothered by someone else's problems. I thought I had enough trouble with my own.

And the night of that afternoon he twisted a bed sheet around his neck, tied it to the highest bar and slowly strangled to death. He jumped down until his body weight caused his homemade noose to cut off his air. And he died.

And a part of me died, too. A part of me that claims to be emotional and caring for other people's plight. It probably makes a lie out of all the things you've seen of me. Maybe I'm not really a GOOD person. Maybe it's just a part of me that is real, but has no feeling. But no, I wouldn't be feeling so fucking guilty right now if I didn't care. Why?? Why didn't I do something? Why didn't I recognize another human being's pain and suffering? I might have been able to help that boy—I'm sure I could have if I'd just taken the time to be civil to him. If I'd not made a judgment on him, an obviously wrong one. It all boils down to the fact that a boy is dead and I am responsible—no, I didn't tell him to end his life—but I

might have been able to help him. I
could have gotten him an appointment
with the psych department. I know how
things work around here—he didn't.
I could have made friends with him,
helped him over the rough spots. But
I didn't. And now he's dead, and so
is a part of me.

[Excerpted from a longer letter that was signed:]

I love you,
Mark

"90 Proof"

Ute Mountain Correctional Facility
Sunday Morning
May 17, 1981

Hello Kid,
     I was driving through life on
flat tires, Mary. Nothing I tried
seemed to work, and I had this monkey
on my back called alcohol to fight
with. It wasn't that I drank TOO
much; it was that I drank constantly,
until my whole life revolved around a
bottle. What few friends I hadn't run
off would laugh behind their hands and
call me a "bottle baby." Booze was
a monster knocking at my back door.
What those friends failed to notice
was that the monster had already
stepped through the door and was there
to stay.
     I want you to understand my
drinking problem, Mary. There was
virtually no time in the day that I
wasn't drinking, or thinking about
drinking. I was known to my neighbors
by a registered trademark: 90 proof.
I carried a glass of scotch to the
shower, to the store, to work, to
answer the front door, to go to the
bathroom, and to the bar. I made sure
that at least a half a glass—drinking

glass—of booze waited for me on the dash board for when the bar closed. I didn't even BREATHE without booze.

I'm talking about YEARS of this. Constantly. I remember that after Cheryl and I moved from Boston to Minneapolis we consumed a fifth a day of Canadian Club whiskey. And that wasn't even a drop in the bucket to what I was drinking behind her back; the quick little snorts from a hidden bottle. I'd stash pints of Vodka everywhere: under the front seat of the car, one in an old purse of Cheryl's, in our chest of drawers, one in a gym locker at Augsburg. I paid $3.15 a month to the recreation fund for that locker just so I could have a bottle at school. That's how serious I was about drinking. You see, it would have taken 3 to 5 minutes to walk out to my car for a snort—this only took time to walk 'cross campus to the gym. Yeah, much more expedient. It's no wonder I never completed a single semester at Augsburg. I wouldn't or couldn't show up for classes, and when I did I was about three sheets to the wind anyway, so I didn't learn much. This was in 1972. (I think.)

One of the prices drinking has levied against me is the loss

of consistent background. There
are shady spots in my life that I
confuse with other times. My memory
plays tricks on me by changing events
and geography and time. I remember
incidents clearly, but sometimes the
location of the event wrong; or the
date is off by as much as two years.
My drinking was the cause of this
shady oblivion.

It's not easy to talk about
this. Having been on the wagon
(imposed) for the last four years,
I am deeply ashamed that I slipped
so far into the bottle. It's not an
easy thing to admit that the last ten
years have been for nothing; that
the profit of a decade could be typed
on a postage stamp. And it's hard
for me to tell you what a failure I
was—perhaps still am—and ask for your
love.

As you read this stuff remember
who I am now. And remember that when
I explain my venture into crime that
I really am not a hideous, malignant
monster just waiting to do evil. Most
of what the papers said was untrue.
They sensationalize the facts to
sell newspapers. I *am* a criminal,
in clinical terms, but not the cold-
blooded killer type who calculatingly
sets up a design for murder. And

remember that we all possess the
ability for homicide. You would know
this first hand—as would I—because
we've tried to kill a human being—
OURSELVES. And that given the correct
set of circumstances the violence we
unleashed on ourselves could easily
have been directed against some
outside influence. I hope it doesn't
sound as if I'm making excuses, Mary.
I've had four years to think of these
things and I think I've viewed them
objectively. (I hope…) I have a
great sense of my inner construction,
and I pretty much know what drives me.
In being honest with you I'm being
honest with me. Don't shut me out
until I finish.
I <u>love</u> you,
ME

Killing a Rabbit

Ute Mountain Correctional Facility
April 25, 1982

Dear Mary,

It must have burrowed under the
fence without setting off any alarms.
Fuzzy white, it hopped up around my
window with its red nose and quivering
whiskers. I called to it and its ears
laid flat on its bunny rabbit head.
Eyes the color of deep charcoal, I
could almost imagine the thoughts
that ran through its mind: "Food"
and "Play" and "Happy." It bounded
this way and that, comfortable in
its freedom of movement, lazy in the
spring sunshine.

And then in a sunny streak
of white, it scrambled and hopped
back out to the fence. Men in blue
uniforms were chasing it. They
couldn't catch it. It dodged, ran,
squirmed and zigzagged its way to the
hole it had made in the fence. I
laughed at the antics of the cops as
they fell and raced around. And I
gave a thankful little prayer when
the bunny got through the fence to
freedom.

It sat on the other side looking

at the men who had chased it.   It
licked its snowy fur and was content
to warm in the sun.   Maybe she was
pregnant.

As she sat watching the man
shout at her she failed to see the
perimeter guard off to her left.   I
think she must have sensed something
just before the man pulled the
trigger, for she jerked her head up,
ears standing tall, and glanced for a
moment at her murderer.   But it was
too late.

The guard picked up what was
left of the rabbit and held it at
arm's length, holding the shotgun
over his head in the universal signal
of victory.   He seemed very proud of
having gunned down a defenseless wood
creature, as if it were a lion or
killer bear he had defeated.   And then
he threw the bunny rabbit in the ditch
and got back in his car.

That scene which played outside
my window deserves comment.   Not for
its recognizable cruelty and obvious
psychological implications, but for
its cultural and social aspects as
well.   Bear with me as I think on
paper and try to reason out why a man
could do such a thing.

He must have had a reason.
We can rule out fear—who could be

afraid of a harmless rabbit? We can probably rule out anger: he had a smile on his face as he pulled the trigger, and he displayed the dead rabbit like a trophy. I think if he were angry he would have kicked the rabbit instead of martyring it. We can assume that the guard felt emotion during the act of cruelty, and after it also. His smile was the smile of accomplishment, the smile that asked his peers to accept him, let him into their social group with the initiation of the killing. Not being a scientist I can't give you empirical evidence that the man's smile represented what I know it did, but I am as sure of that smile as I am of my own name. He sought gratification from the social unit of the guards, much as a convict will do violence to another to gain respect from his peer group in here.

I think that's it. I think he wanted to be noticed, patted on the back; I think he wanted to belong. I wonder at the control he used to shoot the rabbit. I wonder what went through his mind as he made the decision to kill. I wonder if there was confusion over the ethics involved. I wonder if he had doubts after the fact. And most of all, I wonder at the inhumanity

he displayed with his act. The
same inhumanity that is bred by his
working conditions. Had he become
so inured to pain and suffering that
the value of that suffering was less
to him than it was a year ago? Has
his working environment endowed
him with a newfound capacity for
cruelty? Or was he as he now appears
to be: always cruel, dispassionate to
others' feelings? The fact remains
that he took the life of an innocent,
defenseless creature. His motives
appear to be social in design. I must
conclude that his environment (that of
prison) has enabled him, through its
total disregard of ethical standards,
to conceive, decide, and carry out
the violence done to the rabbit. It
would take no great stretch of the
imagination to understand that this
man could just as easily shoot an
unarmed man in prison. It could be
done because the groundwork had been
lain by the destruction of the bunny
rabbit.

Violence is indicative to man's
nature. We <u>fought</u> our way from the
trees, battling animals and nature
and ourselves to get to our present
level of civilization. The dark
side, the side that brought us from
Mesopotamia to the present, has not

been eliminated through the centuries. A part of that dark past struck out at humanity through my own violence. It was not something controllable, not something with an off and on switch. I was transported back to a more primitive time, a time when violence and cruelty was a mark of greatness and not a stain upon the entire race. Perhaps the guard heard the throbbing of the primal drums, too. Who knows? But today's restrictiveness in manner and behavior are foreign and dangerous to man's psyche. We are forced to behave in mores created to give man dignity, but all too often they fail. We lose our independence, our individuality, our creativeness--but we have not lost our aggressiveness, our instincts, our reactions to violence.

End of the Social Psychology lesson for today. Forgive me when I ramble on.

I felt deeply for the rabbit. I felt deeply for the guard. The rabbit I love; the guard I hate.

[Excerpted from a longer letter and signed:]

Keep your wits about you.
I do love you,
Mark

The Influence of Violence

Ute Mountain Correctional Facility
June 1, 1982

Dear Mary,

Keep up the letters. They are
balm to my bruised life. I like to
hear about your days.

Something you might find
interesting. In 1929 a guy named
Alexander Berkman wrote What is
Communist Anarchism? In it he said,
"Wherever you turn you will find that
our entire life is built on violence
or the fear of it. From earliest
childhood you are subjected to the
violence of parents or elders. At
home, in school, in the office,
factory, field, or shops, it is always
someone's authority which keeps you
obedient and compels you to do his
will.

"The right to compel you is
called authority. Fear of punishment
has been made into duty and is called
obedience.

"In this atmosphere of force and
violence, of authority and obedience,
of duty, fear of punishment we all
grow up; we breathe it through our
lives. We are so steeped in the
spirit of violence that we never stop

to ask whether violence is right or wrong. We only ask if it is legal, whether the law permits it."

You see, violence is a part of our lives so deeply ingrained that it is commonplace. Our fear of retribution for not following rules, whether they be rules of behavior or rules of your boss telling you to do something unpleasant, because he hangs your job over your head as the implied threat. And fear of losing your job motivates you to do as he asks—most of the time.

So. The philosophical question of the day is: Do you believe that violence or the threat of violence influences all actions in life? Can you site examples where you acted independently and said to hell with retribution! and did what you wanted? Have you ever defied an authority figure when you had a lot to lose? And finally, do you think this is a good way for human beings to conduct their lives?

If you have time between all the good images you've been writing me try to answer a couple of the questions I've asked in the last few letters. If you have to choose which thing to do in your letters, please, by all means, give me the descriptions

of your life out there. I sometimes
wonder if there are really trees and
bushes and flowers left in the world.
You are really my only contact with
all those real things.
        Talk to you Sunday.

Love,
Mark

This letter to the editor first appeared in <u>The San Juan Journal</u>.

Stop Kicking Us

May 8, 1988

Editor: I get angry when I read the constant public attacks on criminals in the opinion section of your newspaper. I grit my teeth when public reaction to crime forces legislation to increase sentences and build still more prisons.

All these responses to the crime problem are geared to the criminal justice system and disregard the system's people.

We prisoners are people. We are not crazed animals or heinous creatures. Our behavior may have been heinous, our actions may have been shocking, but we remain human beings.

Imprisoning us like the animals you believe us to be is not changing our behavior. More than 70% of us will be back in prison again, simply because we haven't learned to act any differently. Longer sentences in overcrowded warehouses do not force positive behavior changes. Constant punishment, degradation and humiliation are not the oral keystones

on which to build in us a social
conscience.

Stop kicking us. Attack our
behavior with programs to teach us
right ways of thinking. Declare
war on our attitudes and actions by
teaching us marketable job skills and
training our emotions and intellects
to react in socially acceptable ways.
But don't attack us as people, for we
are you.

When chemotherapy is recommended
to kill a single cancerous growth,
doctors do not irradiate the entire
body to get the malignancy. What
corrections needs is a similar
surgical strike that removes the
anti-social behavior but leaves the
surrounding flesh intact.

Mark Thompson #43701
Broken Arrow Correctional Facility

The Catharsis of Writing

Broken Arrow Correctional Facility
August 7, 1990

Dear Mary,

Why don't you write your experiences of 8 years ago? Such a catharsis that is. I ought to know. I wrote out my most pain-filled years and then promptly tore them up--burned them, actually. I didn't write them for anyone, just for me to get it all out. And as I was writing I looked at my every action in another light and found out that yes, I did a terrible thing in 1977, but that no, I am not a terrible person. That was one hell of a revelation to me. Hope I'm not giving advice or anything, I know how you hate that. But we're friends. You can reject anything I say and even call me names if you want, but I figure you respect honesty as much as I do.

Okay, back to writing. It doesn't have to be chronological—I mean it doesn't have to go from point A (the beginning) to point Z (the end). Just sit down and write of perhaps 5 minutes at the hospital, any five minutes. And the next time write of one of the hours. You do

it piece by piece, Pal. In fact, I
know of no writer who writes a book or
story from the beginning to the end in
order. The order comes later, much
later. Just pick a time in your life
in Pueblo and start there. It's good
practice because it teaches you to
think at the same time. It helps you
sort things out and identify all the
excess baggage you carry around. At
least it does for me and every other
writer I've ever read about.

[Excerpted from a longer letter and signed:]

Love,
Mark

I Became A Person

*Excerpt from a letter written to Bill Goodman,
Department of Corrections, after their visit.*

Broken Arrow Correctional Facility
August 6, 1994

Dear Bill,

It is a cycle you know, or maybe
you don't know. The shame of having
killed an innocent human being in a
fit of panic, the grief of his family
like a horrible stench piggybacking
on every thought, every action, every
source within me which no amount of
washing can ever bathe away. The
humiliation of my family, the pain of
his; the hatred of society when they
found me unworthy of life and asked
permission to kill me for my terrible
actions.

I could no longer tolerate the
boy who had killed a man, and I had
not yet reached a maturity and sense
of self which flourished independent of
my own misunderstandings. I studied.
I wrote. I prayed. I contemplated
inner and outer landscapes and built
connections to each. I recognized an
incredible juxtaposition of values
and followed them back to their roots

and yanked them from the soil of
my character. I discarded impure
speculation, defaulting to logic,
asking "what" instead of "why." All
the invented detail of my past was
swept away, and the logic cut a clear
path through the clutter in my mind.
I found and implemented a certain code
of behavior based on morality, not
need. And all the while the prison
environment pursued me like a braying
hound, snapping at the heels of my
newfound Spirit and pausing in the
chase only long enough to lift its leg
and piss on the delicate seedlings in
my new garden of character.

But I won, I beat the odds, I
became a person with whom I could
live, because I grew larger than
myself, eliminating or accepting the
footprints of past indiscretions that
led to forbidden behavior. It took
years.

Thanks for stopping by. I
enjoyed our conversation.

Sincerely,
Mark Thompson

Letter from Cactus County, Texas

In a political move to reduce spending and over-crowded conditions at Broken Arrow Correctional Facility, 520 inmates were shackled and transported 500 miles across state lines where they were housed at the Cactus County Correctional Facility in Texas. This letter, written by Mark Thompson and published in <u>The Desert News</u>, described the desolate boredom in austere conditions.

August 8, 1996

A day in the life of a pod begins at 6 a.m., when the overhead banks of fluorescent lights come on. There are twenty of us in this pod right now, often as many as 24; never fewer than nineteen. We sleep in metal bunk beds less than an arm's reach from each other. The pod is a cement box with a shower and metal toilets at one end, and metal picnic tables in the middle.

The first thing after the lights come on is the Great God Television, that mesmerizing Cyclops that traps so many of the younger ones. Between five and eight of the men have been up all night. They turn the TV to cartoons until I get up and change it to the morning news. We call the nightriders 'bugs.'

Sometime between 6 and 8 a.m. we'll go to breakfast. We dress in our orange pumpkin suits and are escorted to the chow hall. We are told where to sit. We come back and are counted at 7:30. At count times we must stand by our bunks. At 8 a.m., classes are called. We only have one man who goes to GED class. Never mind that he is a mining engineer and 67 years old—when it was learned that he didn't have a GED, they signed him up for classes.

At 8:30, unless it has rained within the last two days or some other arbitrary reason, we can go to yard. The yard is a fenced-in dirt and cement place with one basketball court. They took the weights out after our mini-riot. Yard can last until 10:30. Our mining engineer comes back from GED class (where he has spent a good part of the morning instructing the teacher) about 10:30 as well. All the people in the pod go back to sleep except me.

Between 11:15 and 12:45, we are again marched as a group to the chow hall for lunch and marched back. Count is at 1 p.m. Since no one works in our pod, the afternoons are spent in riotous noise, card-playing, soap operas and talk shows featuring one-legged transvestites who have beefs with their mothers.

Evening chow is between 4:30 and 6:30. Count is at 7 p.m. Lights go out at 10:30 each evening, and the bugs get up. Guards come around at 11 p.m. with hot water (since we have only tepid water in the pod and no electrical hot pots or coffee pots). Most [of the prisoners in the pod] are up and noisy until 1 or 1:30 a.m.; the bugs stay up all night. The television stays on until 3 or 4 each morning. The basic routine is the same seven days a week.

A few words about the people in the pods. Some men bathe regularly and some don't. The oldest is 67, the youngest wasn't born when I first came to prison. The constant droning conversations are often animated and concern only three main topics: cars, crimes or bitches. All women are bitches in these conversations; all cars are fast; all crimes were great, and they wouldn't have gotten caught if somebody—usually a "bitch"—hadn't set them up or ratted on them.

The time in here is hard, slow, redundant, unfulfilling. There is no privacy. Ever. Conflicts flare and die down quickly.

Mostly we are defeated.

Thoughts on 9/11

This text was copied from an e-mail exchange Mark had with his nephew Justin in the aftermath of September 11th. Although Mark was out of prison and on parole when he wrote these words it is important to remember that the attack of 9/11 impacted everyone, including the unseen and forgotten who live in locked places.

The men and women living in a separate and brutal society that is often invisible yet still within the border and very much a part of the United States.

September 13, 2001

Justin wrote:

The truth hurts but its gotta be done. We didn't retaliate when they bombed it the first time or when they bombed the Olympics or anything else and now it's time we stop talkin' and start kickin' some ass.

Mark replied:

After careful thought, Justin, and not from anger. Evil is never defeated by using greater evil. I don't know the answers, but I do know that wiping out bits of humanity because we're grieving is what we've always done and it's never worked. It's a lot easier to hurt people than

to understand them and negotiate
with them. It's always been easier
to conquer than to cooperate. We're
all angry and hurt, the whole country
is. But striking out when we've been
hurt is only one option, and usually
not the best. If the Hawks (the
Republicans and the religious right)
have their way they would make this
a Jihad, a religious war, and when
we've eliminated the Muslims, will we
go after Jews? Or even other sects
of Christianity that the ruling class
doesn't like? Be careful, Nephew,
responding with your pain and anger.
Think first. I will respect your
opinion, but not until you've thought
through the consequences. You see,
if this escalates, it might be you
who joins up and goes to the desert
to kill human beings or be killed
yourself. Taking human life is wrong.
Taking human life because we're mad or
hurt is evil. I love you.

My Thoughts Fall into Holes

Five years after his near-fatal suicide attempt, when Mark's brain function was gradually returning, he wrote this letter.

Kiowa Correctional Facility
August 28, 2009

Dear Mary,

There may be one more letter left in this pen, my favorite. It is quite illegal and was obtained nefariously, as are most things of value in this cement garden.

I would be honored to write a testimonial for you. You do know that writing long and understandable sentences is often beyond my ability, because my thoughts start out guns a blazin' heading toward the center of the sentence where the verb explodes into action, and suddenly a hole appears, slanting downward, slippery, and I cannot escape its vacant beckoning. I am consumed. I come out the other end of the hole in my brain and wonder where I've been, what I might have said or meant, but there's no comfort in my thoughts, just more holes strewn about.

I think that's why I write

poetry now. Poetry seems to me to be complicated thoughts and sentences with intentional holes pounded through them. My guess is that the reader is intended to fill in the holes with fragments of her own life, thereby internalizing the meaning. Anyway, I tried writing around the holes, but the holes are tricky, deceptive things that spring up at their own rate and cause my thoughts to fall through them. Kind of like now. I had something to say to you, but it fell down a hole. Let me see what I can do for your testimonial.

Ann Rand gave crisp advice to writers like me who are trying to put the fractured pieces of our lives back together through writing. She said, "Don't ask, what do I need to do?" She said, "Instead, when tackling any problem, ask 'What is the nature of the thing I wish to do?'" In other words, don't look inside for answers, look outside. And that's pretty much how I found poetry—It's the perfect box to drop my thoughts into.

More Later,
Mark

In Love

Kiowa Correctional Facility
September 28, 1980

Good Morning, My Dear Lady,

I wish letters would go out
on Saturdays, I've never in my life
wished to communicate with anyone more
than I do you.
So? You float up to the clouds
when you read my letters. To me
that simple sentence is worth more
than publishing two major novels
and getting worldwide recognition.
Sometimes I think the ability to
express thanks and feeling is a lost
art in letter writing. You do it so
well. I had to sit back and take
two humble pills and smile inside of
myself. Thank you for making me feel
that I have worth in this world. You
are important, and if I can reach you,
then most of my goals have been met.
You said that my words caress
that part of you which so desperately
needs attention. I know what it's
like to have volumes of honest love
inside of me, just waiting to be
given to someone. I know what it's
like to possess the tenderness and
yearning of an open heart. I know

how much the small and simple, almost
subconscious gestures of two people
sharing a healthy love can mean; like
the right words in times of hurt,
a tender caress and a gentle kiss
in unpredictable moments. A quick
smile, for no reason, and finding the
one you love staring at you with that
same love when you are not looking;
catching them loving you. I miss
looking into the depths of my love's
eyes and finding her total being
reflected in open and unafraid trust.
I miss the feeling of that unnameable
bond that lovers enjoy; the bond that
can stretch distances and time and
still be totally secure. And I so
miss the completeness two people can
share, both in mind and body. The
union of forces strong enough to last
out all weather.

     The emptiness and longing inside
of me is a physical thing, a warm
cancer that eats into my entirety.
And I recognize that longing in you,
Mary. That feeling, just below the
surface that's like not eating for a
whole day, but it's your soul, not
your belly.

     I love you for showing and
sharing your depth with me.

     You remind me of a kitten, all
furry and purry but with those sharp

little kitten-claws just beneath the surface.

Thank you for making me feel that I am important to someone. You have a way of telling me that I have worth to someone besides myself.

[Excerpted from a 12-page letter and signed:]

With Love,
Mark

Acknowledgments

My deepest appreciation and gratitude go out to the people who have believed in me and helped me heal and transform my life through the power of written words.

To the real man behind the name "Mark Thompson" who knew, thirty-three years ago, that there were unseen and unformed books inside of me.

To my writing coach, editor and publisher Stewart S. Warren at Mercury HeartLink for his words of encouragement that kept me searching deep and reaching high for what really needed to be said. For his Eagle vision when I was lost in my own Mouse vision. And for those wonderful "Oh, Yeah!" moments of clarity and insight that brought the next step into focus.

To my dear friend Rhonda Ashurst for believing in this book, for walking the road beside me—both literally and figuratively—and for having a good sense of a well-told story.

To members of *The Sophia Writers Circle*: Rhonda Ashurst, Holly Felmlee and Lisa Marlin for the creative inspiration that we have shared, nurtured and grown through trusted friendships.

To readers of drafts who offered invaluable insights and helpful criticisms: Rhonda Ashurst, Judith Burrell, Miles Eddy, Holly Felmlee, Peter Van Pelt, and

Katherine Park Woolbert.

To my friend and partner Miles Eddy for his emotional and financial support through difficult times that allowed me to pursue my vision.

To the Reverend Katherine Griffis for introducing me to Howard Zehr's Restorative Justice work.

To Katherine Park Woolbert who applied her Creative Writing and English teacher expertise to my final draft.

To my parents the Reverend W. Austin Van Pelt, Ph.D. and Elenor K. Van Pelt whose lives have been dedicated to social justice, human rights, and caring for others.

To the people who gather weekly around the recovery table: you have helped me understand that letting go doesn't mean to stop caring; it means I can't do it for someone else. You have offered me countless insights into what it means to love an alcoholic while maintaining my balance, health and sanity.

My prison and social justice work has also been influenced by these courageous authors: Michelle Alexander, *The New Jim Crow: Mass Incarceration in an Age of Colorblindness*; Asha Bandele, *The Prisoner's Wife: A Memoir*; Demetria Martinez, *Mother Tongue*; Sister Helen Prejean, *Dead Man Walking*; and Howard Zehr, *The Little Book of Restorative Justice*.

About the Author

Mary Elizabeth Van Pelt is a humanitarian devoted to social change. She worked for twenty years in the field of Human Services but has come to rely more on individuals and grassroots organizations than on the current system of using government funds to solve social issues. The author believes in Restorative Justice, a process that involves, to the extent possible, the individuals who have been hurt by a crime—the offender, the victim and other stake holders. The criminal justice system focuses on punishment; Restorative Justice works to heal and restore the web of damaged relationships.

Van Pelt's first book, *In Silence I Speak: My Journey through Madness*, is a memoir about outgrowing the services that the mental health system offers. It is also published by Mercury HeartLink. The author makes her home in the San Luis Valley of Southern Colorado near the Rio Grande. Her rural neighbors include deer, hawk, raven and an occasional glimpse of the red fox.

www.maryvanpelt.com